AWKWARD QUESTIONS ON CHRISTIAN LOVE

HUGH MONTEFIORE comes from an Anglo-Jewish family and became a Christian while at Rugby School. He was a scholar of St. John's College, Oxford, but had his university career interrupted by five years' war service. He trained for the Ministry at Westcott House, Cambridge, where he later returned as Principal. He was Fellow and Dean of Gonville and Caius College for nine years, and University Lecturer in the New Testament. He became Vicar of the University Church of Great St. Mary's in October, 1963, and is a Canon Theologian of Coventry Cathedral. He has contributed to recent Cambridge theological writing, including chapters in A. R. Vidler's *Soundings* and the Fontana *God, Sex and War*.

HUGH MONTEFIORE

Awkward Questions
on
Christian Love

Collins
FONTANA BOOKS

First published in Fontana Books 1964

CONTENTS

PREFACE

The contents of this book were prepared for this year's Lincoln Lectures, which are given annually during Passion Week at the Bishop's Hostel, Lincoln. I am grateful to the Principal, Canon Alan Webster, for having invited me to give them, and I am honoured to be included in the distinguished succession of earlier lecturers, many of whom have published more profound contributions than these.

I have taken this theme of "Awkward Questions on Christian Love" because of my belief that it is far better to face awkward questions about one's faith (even if one cannot answer them) than to ignore them. I have selected certain aspects of Christian love because many people to-day fear that the Christian claim that "God is love" is denied by the facts of human existence, by certain well-known formulations of Christian doctrine, by the practice of the Christian Church—yes, and even by certain facets of the Gospels themselves.

I have covered far too much ground far too quickly to do full justice to the questions that I have raised. The Problem of Evil, the Perfection of Jesus, the Meaning of the Event of Christ, the Christian Ideal of Neighbourly Love —however ineptly handled, these are vast and tremendous themes!

St. Augustine wrote thirteen books on the single subject of the Doctrine of the Trinity, " lest nothing be said ". Although these four short lectures are by comparison like mice to a mountain, I have published them for precisely the same reason, " lest nothing be said ". If professional theologians do not write more popular theology, others must attempt it, for the need is urgent.

Epiphany 1964   *Hugh Montefiore*

1. *THE GREAT ACCUSATION*

This course of Passiontide lectures is about four aspects of the love of God. But I must not presume on my subject. It is by no means self-evident either that God exists, or, if he does, that his nature is love. The bland assurance by many Christians that of course God is loving is a major cause of stumbling to many agnostics. So far as blandness is concerned, my sympathies lie with the agnostics.

I cannot commit myself to a belief in God until I know roughly what I mean by that three-letter word. To a large extent the matter turns on what is meant by God. The inmost nature of the Divine Being is bound to be mysterious to mortal men; but if we can give *no meaning at all* to the word God, then we have no further need of the hypothesis. Many people have their own private notion of God. For myself, I am content to understand the word God approximately in the sense of traditional Christian theism.

Why do I believe in him? I can offer no proof, only the grounds of my faith. I am not of course conscious of these grounds when I commit myself to God: an act of faith looks forward to its object, not backward to its roots. Yet the grounds of my belief are none the less real for that.

When I look at the world (both the inanimate world and the world of human beings), I find within it too much evidence of mind and purpose to be able to believe that the whole universe is "random" and devoid of ultimate meaning. Furthermore I have, in some measure, experienced the "Other" in the midst of life, so that this has become part of myself. For me to say that this experience is illusory would be to deny myself. I find, too, that the deepest need of every man is to know that he is a child of God; and I do not see how man could have developed this need unless it were grounded in reality.

Of course there are reasons, too, which lead me, at any rate with the "top of my mind", to doubt God's existence. There is the amazing success of the natural and social sciences in explaining (very quickly too) how things and people work without bringing in God; there is the vastness of the universe and the smallness of man; and there is the apparent silence (should I say indifference?) of his problematical Creator.

Yet, despite all this, I am bound to seek a

reason for all things. My mind will not rest ultimately in anything but rationality and unification. Since I cannot find in the universe the cause of its own existence, I must believe in God who created it and who sustains it in being, and who gives it life. Since God cannot have created something greater than himself, his nature cannot be less than personal being, which is the highest form of life of which man can have experience. I may make these inferences about the nature of God's being, but all that I can experience of God are his effects. I cannot know him in himself.

By this affirmation of traditional Christian theism, I am setting my face against certain forms of continental Protestantism which believe God to be "wholly other" than his creation. Since I believe that God is infinite and eternal, I cannot accept that any part of his created universe can exist "below" or "above" or "outside" or "beyond" him. As St. Paul (as well as a pagan poet) is reported to have said: "In him we live and move and have our being." In mediaeval terms we might say that our being participates in the Being of God. In the words of poetry, God is nearer than seeing, closer than breathing.

On the other hand if traditional theism is opposed to the idea of an absolutely transcendent

God, it is equally opposed to that of a purely immanentist deity. The Bishop of Woolwich was wise to consider carefully "the suspicion of pantheism which must doubtless cling to any reconstruction that questions the existence of God as a separate Being".[1] But the Bishop is, in my judgement, equally foolish to think that he can adequately "rebut" such a suspicion. It is impossible to "translate" traditional theism into adequate and acceptable modern imagery without some doctrine of creation. If God is not separate from his creation, there cannot be, strictly speaking, any creation at all. "God in the depths of our being" or "God as the ultimate ground of existence" or "ultimate reality" (whatever these phrases actually mean) become part of the universe. The substitution of personal for mechanistic or organic categories does not alter the fundamentally pantheistic character of such a viewpoint. Pantheism may give an explanation of existence, in as much as existence itself becomes deified. But it cannot adequately explain moral struggle, and it is absolutely incompatible with the belief that "God is love", since what is evil as well as what is good must be regarded as divine. (It is perhaps significant that, while *Honest to God* contains plenty of

[1] *Honest To God,* 1963, p. 130.

assertions that God is love, there is no attempt
in the book to grapple with the problems which
this assertion raises.) Moreover, if God is not
separable from his universe, there must have
been a time when God was not—unless, of course,
matter is eternal, in which case the personal
ground of all existence must have spent infinite
time in impersonal torpor.

In contrast to views of pure immanence or
pure transcendence, I understand by the word
GOD the infinite personal Being in whom we
all live and move and have our being, and whose
divine activity we experience as the Creator and
Sustainer of all things. I have said what I understand by the word God, not that I understand
God himself. Any attempt to define God or
to describe him makes an object of him, reduces
him to "one of a kind", betrays his absolute
uniqueness. The reality of God shows all our
mental images of him to be but idols, reduces all
our theology to straw—useful straw, but still
straw. His nature remains immeasurably mysterious; but I have experienced enough of his
activity to be assured of his existence.

To affirm the existence of God is one thing:
to assert that his nature is love is quite different.
It is not enough to say that God's nature is revealed in the love of Jesus.

> *Now Barabbas was a killer*
>   *And they let Barabbas go,*
> *But you are being crucified*
>   *For nothing here below;*
> *While God is up in heaven,*
>   *But he doesn't do a thing,*
> *With a million angels watching*
>   *And they never move a wing.*

The ballad is a protest against the difference between the character of Jesus and the character of God. For we may grant that Jesus showed perfect love operative in human personality; we may grant too that the love of Jesus rescues us from evil; but we still have to explain the existence of those evils which engulfed Jesus himself and from which he has rescued us. For God is the Creator and Sustainer of all that is evil as well as all that is good. Only if we vindicate him as Creator can we accept him as the Father of our Lord Jesus Christ.

If there is evil in the universe, we can regard either God as ultimately responsible for it, or (if we believe in his existence) the Devil. In fact the introduction of the Devil solves nothing. For if the Devil is responsible for evil, but subordinate to God, then we must ask ourselves, "Why is the Devil evil?" just as we had earlier to ask ourselves, "Why are people or things evil?" We have merely removed the problem one stage further back. If on the other hand we regard the Devil as ultimately responsible for evil, then God is no longer God. He is no longer the Creator and Sustainer of all things, since the Devil lies outside his creative and sustaining power. To postulate an eternal Devil in permanent opposition to God does not resolve our problem, for the mind cannot rest in an eternal dualism.

If then we believe in God, we must accept that he is ultimately responsible for all that is evil. We cannot wash our hands of this agonising problem. In a vastly popular little book Dr. Whale has written, " There is no adequate answer to this problem along purely intellectual terms."[2] And he continues in words which may bring comfort to the heart of the pragmatic Englishman, but which can hardly satisfy his head: " The real issue of life can be solved only in terms of life's experience, and not of any intellectual theory."

It is true that a Christian can never claim that he fully understands the mysterious relationship in which the created universe stands to its Creator. There is bound to be a very great deal about which the Christian should properly remain agnostic. Moreover the Christian will expect his experience of life to confirm his innermost convictions. Who but a madman would

[2] *The Problem of Evil* (1936), p. 10.

continue indefinitely to hold convictions which were consistently and permanently contradicted by life's experience? So far we may agree with Dr. Whale.

Yet when we are considering the problem of evil we are dealing with the greatest of all difficulties which lie in the way of theistic belief. For we can only give our heart's adoration to Him whom we acknowledge as morally and spiritually superior. We can only worship Him whom we judge worthy of it. The existence of evil raises the question whether God is worthy of worship. Just because the problem of evil poses a *moral* accusation against God, its force presses home on us harder than any other.

In all matters of religious belief we attempt to give an intelligent and intelligible explanation of our belief. Our motto, like that of Anselm, might well be "faith seeking understanding". Even if we do not know the answer to a problem of belief, yet we believe that there is an answer. But here, at this crucial point, where the Great Accusation is laid against God, we are so often content to pretend both that there is no answer and that it doesn't matter that there isn't. We are of course sympathetic about the catastrophes which strike down other people, especially those which impress us by their size or which afflict defenceless people or intimate friends; whole populations starving through drought or warfare; a doomed infant shrieking away its life through some incurable illness; a child born with a twist to his mind or rendered permanently unresponsive by the negligence or the cruelty of parents. "It's horrible," we tell ourselves, "it's unspeakable. Even though we must accept these things, they are evil, and God cannot possibly approve of them." We forget all too easily that even if God did not design these things, he permits them. How easy it is to say: "The world is full of evils and yet God is the God of love. These two don't seem to fit, but the problem is too much for me, and it doesn't really matter."

But it does matter, terribly. Problems of faith are never soluble by logical proof. But faith must seek understanding; and unless Christians are prepared to tackle the problem of evil in all its intensity, and unless they can begin to see a way through the problem, they have no right whatsoever to claim that theirs is a reasonable belief. And if a belief is not held to be reasonable, there is no reason why it should be held.

Christians far too seldom realise what a strong case can be made for regarding God as the Devil, "the Cosmic Sadist, the spiteful imbecile." We find ourselves in a universe where we cannot be sure whether there is any ultimate purpose and meaning. Who but the Devil could have left us in such suspense? Who but the Devil would have created a universe with such a wasteful evolutionary system? From this evolutionary system man has emerged as a result of struggle and competition, so that competitiveness has become built into his nature; and having emerged triumphant as lord of nature, man is then commanded to deny his nature and to be humble and cooperative. Who but the Devil could arrange that? How can a God of love expect man to be loving when he has emerged from a system based on predation? What kind of Creator is responsible for the complex cycle of the malarial parasite whose very existence is dependent on human destruction? Parents naturally implant in their infants' minds the seeds from which later grow a belief in the fatherly providence of God; but how can this belief be compatible with natural catastrophes, mental and physical pain, gross physical disability or spiritual incapacity, whether it be derived from parents or caused by environment?

As man considers the long list of his frustrations, so his accusations against God increase in number and gravity. Man is given a method of reproduction that is exquisitely pleasurable: who but the Devil would demand strict continence in its use? On the other hand to endow man with aspirations of goodness and integrity which he can never achieve might well seem more cruel than kind. Who but the Devil could build into man a consuming desire for happiness, and at the same time contrive that, if happiness becomes the deliberate aim of life, it is impossible of achievement? Or again, God implants in man natural and instinctive fears, and yet at the same time he commands man to be loving and trustful. Lack of self-awareness commonly results in mental or emotional imbalance; yet God has omitted to give us a ready means of discovering, and thus of liberating, these buried feelings and sentiments. Man is surrounded by the bounty of nature and is endowed with sufficient intelligence to understand nature and to manipulate it. Who but the Devil could give all this and yet withhold the moral power to prevent its destructive use? Who but the Devil would implant in man a hearty desire to pray, and then often apparently ignore his prayers? Man inherits a strong unconscious instinct for life which makes him usually fight hard against death even when its advent would be kind. At the same time man has a consuming fear of annihilation, and lacks a natural assurance of continued existence after death. Who but the Devil could create man for eternity and omit to apprise him of this fact?

God has given us no natural knowledge of our origin, nature or future. He has put men into a world without telling them the purpose of life on this planet, and has left them to find out for themselves what its probable end will be. Even if the Creator assures us of his presence, he can withdraw that assurance at a peak period of crisis. " My God," cried Jesus at the moment of greatest need, " My God, why hast thou forsaken me?" Has God forgotten to be kind and has his mercy clean gone for ever? Or, has he never been kind at all? " My real fear is not of materialism. If it were true, we— or what we mistake for we—could get out, get from under the harrow. An overdose of sleeping pills would do it. I am more afraid that we are really rats in a trap. Or, worse still, rats in a laboratory. Someone said, I believe, " God always geometrises ". Suppose the truth were " God always vivisects "?[3]

This string of blasphemous accusation gives the impression of a release of pent-up resentment. Intentionally so. For man reacts personally to misfortune and frustration. Even though his reactions may be hidden beneath exterior calm and self-control, they are no less real and no less strong than if they had been vented in rage and hate. Yet once they have been recognised,

[3] N. W. Clerk, *A Grief Observed,* (1961), p. 26.

they can be accepted; and once they have been accepted, it is possible to reason about them. To this let us now turn.

It is not difficult to understand why physical accidents are inevitable in any kind of conceivable physical universe. For matter consists of energy organised according to its own principles of being. The various sciences have had a run of astonishing success in breaking down the fundamental structures of matter, and in making models of molecular structures or minute entities. Thus we now know not only about the system and structure of the atom, but also about the composition of proteins and other complex small entities. After spectacular success in physics, interest is now shifting towards chemistry and biochemistry. More and more structures and systems are being investigated and explained.

It is a fundamental aspect of the physical world that these countless organisations of matter are bound to meet and interact. Without such interaction there could be no change other than mere universal expansion and contraction. Structures of matter are bound to collide with one another, whether it be atom with atom, molecule with molecule, or stuff with stuff. Matter modifies or maintains its form and builds up its structure according to its principles of being. Thus air can turn into water, as the structure of the former becomes modified; or a plant grows and maintains its structure through food proper to its nature. Structures of matter are bound to collide with one another, and as a result of this collision, one particular structure changes another by engulfing it or by submitting to it or by mutual modification. Thus a cat, in swallowing a mouse, engulfs it and breaks down the constituents of the mouse and absorbs into its own system what is useful for the maintenance of its life. The cat has engulfed the mouse, while the mouse has submitted to the cat. On the other hand if a cat fights with a dog, each might leave on the other lasting marks of the encounter: one system has modified the other. The same principles apply to matter at the inorganic as well as the complex organic level. One star can engulf or submit to another or they can modify each other without losing identity. If it were not so there would be no change. But the physical universe is so constituted that change is continuous. Without change, there could be no possibility of regress or progress. Either the physical world would have had to be created so that movement (including progress) was completely unnecessary, or it would have been incapable of fulfilling the purpose for which it was created.

Another basic aspect of the material world is its regularity of operation. Events do not happen arbitrarily; they have a cause. The basic presupposition of natural science is that all physical phenomena are capable of explanation. All changes in the material world are therefore in principle predictable, since there is nothing arbitrary about either the interaction of systems or the results of the interaction which causes change.

It is the combination of interaction of systems on the one hand and regularity of operation on the other hand that makes physical accident possible. Since whatever is regular is predictable in principle, all physical accidents could in principle be avoided with sufficient intelligence, knowledge, forethought and expertise.

Any divine interference either with the natural interaction of systems or with their regularity of operation would be likely to cause in the long run more inconvenience than convenience. At least we now know what is likely to happen. This makes possible personal and civilised life. Divine interference would introduce an arbitrary note into existence which would destroy such security as we have. In any case divine interference, while benefiting some, might do more harm to others.

Despite the regularities of existence, there is a random element built into life. One is tempted

to ascribe this random element to particular opera-
tions of divine providence. This temptation must
be resisted, for it operates within statistically
predictable limits. It is precisely this random
element which has made possible the development of living organisms through the combination of genetic mutation and natural selection.
Slight alterations occur in the structures of individuals in a species. Most of these alterations are useless, and may well be an impediment
for the individual concerned. But from time to
time an alteration will occur which makes an
individual more fitted to survive; and through the
operation of natural selection this characteristic
will in time become dominant throughout the
species. Children born with crippled minds and
crippled bodies may well evoke in us sentiments
of horror and compassion; but without the possibility of these physical aberrations there would
have been no possibility of the evolution of
homo sapiens at all.

It is well known that man emerged from the
evolutionary process after millennia of what now
looks like trial and error. The randomness of
the process results in the evolution of apparently
pointless species, while the operation of natural
selection ensures the continuance of nature's
prodigality. The more of a species that exists,
the more likely that some will survive. And so for

the most part only those species have survived which can reproduce themselves on a grand scale. Without waste, there would be no men.

Already many of the Divine Accusations seem to have been explained. The natural occurrence of drought or famine, earthquake or lightning may seem contrary to what we would expect in a loving Creator; but if he is to create a physical world at all, are not these inevitable? There cannot but be physical accidents. There cannot but be waste on a grand scale. Regularities of life must operate consistently or not at all. If there is to be change, there must be change for the worse as well as for the better. If we are to have a physical universe, these things are inevitable. *Yet they are not thereby justified.*

Pain is as inevitable as accident in a physical world. It is a signal, suited to animal nature, that something is wrong. It is a warning sign of danger; and if it is to operate efficiently, it must operate consistently. Pain caused by illness or disease gives the possibility of remedial treatment and cure. Pain caused by one animal to another is not the result of cruelty, for animals are incapable of cruelty in the sense of conscious deliberate infliction of pain on another living being. They do not act deliberately, but innocently. They do not act from spite but from self-love. If they did not act thus, their species would not have survived.

Pain, as Austin Farrer has remarked, awakens the compassion of fellow-creatures.[4] Why, he asks, does not God prevent what men mitigate? He suggests that perhaps one of the reasons for pain is to awaken compassion among creatures. But Divine Compassion cannot only be operative when there is suffering: it must operate always or not at all. The Creator has presumably ordained pain because it is suited to animal existence. Without it, man would not have emerged from the evolutionary process.

Pain is certainly a vital aspect of animal consciousness as constituted. But God is not thereby absolved from responsibility for creating a universe, or creating the conditions from which a universe could evolve, in which animals have to suffer pain if they are to be animals. In the same way, although physical accidents are inevitable in a physical universe, God is not thereby absolved from responsibility for creating the conditions in which physical accidents can occur, especially as they sometimes have disastrous consequences for his creatures.

It is true that some human pain is deserved; that some human pain can be transcended; and that some human pain is redeemed. But there

[4] *Love Almighty and Ills Unlimited* (1962), p. 104.

are cases when human pain has caused the degeneration of human personality; and sometimes analgesics, rightly used to reduce pain, result in the reduction of human people to almost animal level. Pain could not even be justified on the grounds that it could be proved that it always does people good. In fact there is good evidence that it can do real harm.

And so, although we can show that these ills are necessary for the world as constituted, *we have not yet absolved God from responsibility for them.*

In addition to physical accident and physical pain, men suffer from inner frustrations which lead on the one hand to the commission of all seven deadly sins, and on the other hand to mental maladjustments and affective disorders. These bring estrangement from God, and this estrangement is sin. The cause of sin was thought by our grandparents to be due to the Devil. But, as we have already seen, the introduction of the Devil solves no problem, and, even if we were to admit his existence, we would merely find the same problem of evil at one further remove. According to traditional belief, the Devil tempted Eve, and Eve tempted Adam, and Adam fell, and the infection spread to the whole human race which is descended from Adam and Eve. This primitive myth, while it contains some spiritual truths, does not help in any way to explain the origin of evil. For it is absolutely unhistorical. Adam and Eve never existed. *Homo sapiens* has descended from apelike ancestors. If there was no primal man, there was no primal sin to entail its taint on all posterity.

How then account for the origin of evil and sin? Some are content to regard the Fall merely as a true myth about human nature. "We cannot go further beyond this myth," wrote Brunner.[5] Yet if Christianity is to be regarded as a reasonable faith, some explanation must be given of our basic human condition. Any theory of an actual precosmic fall is unevidenced. In any case sin starts in man. Physical objects and animal life may incline men towards sin; but they cannot be evil in themselves. Atoms or animals are not responsible for their actions. It is because man is a moral being that he is capable of evil. It is because he is responsible for his actions that he is able to commit deliberate sins. Although good actions are intermingled with bad, man is predisposed to be selfish. This is because he has evolved from animals, and inherits their animal nature. An animal that preys on another cannot be accused of acting

[5] E. Brunner, *The Divine Imperative* (E. T., 1937), p. 606.

cruelly or evilly (although their Creator can
be accused of permitting an evolutionary system
in which animals are bound to be predatory).
If animals were not selfish, they would not have
survived. The same is true of babies. A new-
born baby, despite its colossal potentialities, in
many ways resembles an animal. In animals and
babies the instincts express themselves innocently.
But in self-conscious, rational, responsible moral
beings who are capable of choice and self-control,
selfishness becomes evil. I cannot do better than
cite the late Dr. F. R. Tennant, who has seldom
received the attention that is his due. " ' The way
from nature to character ', he wrote, ' is laborious
and full of effort.' Morality consists in the forma-
tion of the non-moral material of nature into
character, in subjecting ' the seething and tumul-
tuous life of natural tendency, of appetite and
passion, affection and desire ', to the moulding
influence of reflective purpose. Here, and not
in any universal and hereditarily transmitted
disturbance of man's nature, is to be found the
occasion or source of universal sinfulness."[6]

Against the view that sin has its origin in our
animal nature is usually brought the objection
that sin's stronghold is in the mind and the
imagination and the will rather than in animal

[6] *The Origin and Propagation of Sin* (Cambridge,
1902), p. 107.

appetites and passions. Tennant himself has been often accused of ignoring the typical *locus* of sin in his attempted explanation of its origin. It is therefore worth quoting Tennant's footnote:

> In the account given here of the development of sin in the individual the " raw material of morality " has been spoken of as if it consisted merely of what is supplied by sensibility. This, however, has been only for simplicity and convenience' sake. Of course the human instincts and impulses do not remain blind when rational life has become developed. Thought transmutes them and makes them but centres of " a complex of associated ramifications due to our richer life ". " Hunger and love " may be the two root elements of human nature, the rockbed of morals. But reason gives greater scope for selfishness than mere instinct, and enormously extends the field which morality has to conquer. It too, no less than sensibility, has to be moralised and yields the stuff from which sin is made.[7]

While the *locus* of sin is not in the animal nature, it is from man's animal nature that it has been derived. Indeed, it is hard to delineate precisely between animal and *homo sapiens*. Extrapolate on the graph from virus to baboon, and you

[7] *Ibid.*, p. 107, note.

get a man. The mind can be controlled far more than we like to admit by unconscious sentiments. Reasoning is often a rationalisation of unconscious desires or fears. A man's judgement and choice can be affected by his emotions and by his instincts. There is nothing good and bad about intellect in itself, but about the use to which the personality puts the intellect, either consciously or unconsciously. Man may be at the mercy of his inner drives which themselves are derived from his animal past. He can be freed from enslavement to these in as much as he realises his nature as a moral being capable of rational and intelligent choice.

Man is not hereby absolved from all responsibility for sin; for he has a degree of genuinely free choice. When he deliberately chooses that which he knows to be wrong he is still responsible for his actions, even if his responsibility has been diminished by the effect on his personality of his evolutionary past. Much of the evil and much of the suffering in the world is caused by the deliberate choices of individuals. This does not however absolve God from responsibility for creating the conditions in which such evil and suffering takes place.

We must therefore lay at God's door this responsibility. Temple said that sin was too probable not to have happened.[8] In fact, sin was absolutely inevitable and God, since he has forethought, must have known this from all eternity. It is impossible to imagine a world in which men could have emerged from an evolutionary process without " original sin ".

Why did God create a world like this? How can we, despite the kind of world in which we live, still think of the Creator as the Father of our Lord Jesus Christ? He is ultimately responsible for physical accident, animal pain, human sin and frustration: how then can he be infinitely loving? Why is he not the Devil? There is no real refuge for the Christian apologist in the mystery of divine choice. He can say, and rightly say, that God creates as he wills. God certainly had an infinity of choices for possible creation. Why he chose one rather than another is beyond the wit of human beings. The clay cannot question the Potter's choice.

But the clay can and does question the Potter about the merits of the universe he did choose. Some semblance of an answer may and must be given.

If God is pure love, then the only reason for the creation of the conditions in which a universe can evolve must be the emergence of beings fit to share in God's love and in God's enjoyment

[8] *Nature, Man and God* (1934), p. 366.

of his universe. God could have created, had he willed to do so, pure spiritual beings whose nature was such that they had to adore him and enjoy his creation. He could have produced this kind of adoration by spiritual automation. But this would not result in true love or true happiness. Such beings could not share in his love and his joy, for they would not be fitted to give or receive these. God wanted the response of free beings. Love that is enforced is not true love at all. Response that is automatic cannot express true happiness or true responsibility. God wishes to attract people to himself by the power of his love. God wishes to win the love of men and women despite the overhang of their evolutionary past, and despite the effect of this past upon their whole personalities. In order to be able to share in God's love, man must be capable of making a free, deliberate and responsible choice to respond to his Creator. The evolutionary system itself has evolved by a kind of natural necessity, but out of this necessity man has emerged with the possibility of exercising responsible freedom. Seen from a human point of view, there would appear to be no means other than the evolutionary system for the creation of this possibility. And it is a real possibility. Decisions are not all predetermined. Men can exercise the power of free and rational choice. They can be free to respond (or to refuse to respond) to God's love. According to the Christian view, in this world they can only begin to respond. Before them lie the endless potentialities of eternal life.

If the evolutionary system exists so that moral beings may evolve who are capable of sharing in the divine love and joy, some kind of explanation that is compatible with a loving Creator can be given of all the pain, waste, evil, frustration and sin in the universe. Such an explanation is neither shallow nor superficial. Sin is not explained away. The evils of the universe are made no less evil; but they subserve a far far greater good. As for those who are casualties in the process, we simply do not know their fate. If however we believe that God is love, we can rest assured that whatever happens to them will be the loving fate for them. Moreover, when we fall victims on the way to pain and suffering, evil and sin, we are comforted by the knowledge that we arouse the Divine Compassion. Christians believe that the Creator is the Father of our Lord Jesus Christ. The sympathy and gentleness of Jesus towards sinners, together with his sense of outrage against sin and sickness, is for them a mirror of the mind of his heavenly Father. If God is responsible for the ills of life, they must cause him pain and compassion when they afflict

the creatures of his love. Like son, like father.
God endures the pain of those ills for which he
is himself responsible in order to create the possibility of the greatest good. The Surgeon, we
believe, is genuinely afflicted in his patients—
and has himself undergone the knife.

We now can begin to see that the whole process
produces beings capable of sharing in God's love
and joy. Perhaps, in the process of the argument,
our notion of God's love may have changed. If
such terrible evil and pain and suffering is to
be endured so that some men may be fitted
to share in the Divine Charity, there is a certain
ruthlessness about God's love which is not usually
associated with the more sentimental conceptions
of charity. God's purpose in creation is to share
his love with his creatures. The process of creation
involves the inevitability of evil. For this God
is responsible. He does not choose certain persons
from the process and fit them for glory, and leave
the rest fitted for destruction. He does not inter-
fere with social conditioning.[9] He reveals himself within the process, but he does not direct it,
or manipulate it.

[9] Sociological research has made nonsense of certain
traditional expressions of the doctrine of election.
There are more women than men in our churches,
but it is exceedingly improbable that God would
elect predominantly middle-class females to be fitted
for glory and leave males of the working class to be
fitted for destruction.

God helps us by his grace when we turn to him, and it is through his goodness that we can turn to him at all; but he allows us to make our own responsible choices, and we can only make these choices to the extent that we are free and responsible and aware of what we are choosing.

No argument can *prove* that God is love. To an unbeliever our reasoning will seem unconvincing, since he can explain the evolutionary system to his satisfaction in a different way without God. Belief in God is a matter of faith, not of proof. The most that a man can do about intellectual objections to his faith is to satisfy himself that there are reasonable grounds for his belief (although these reasonable grounds are seldom themselves the real grounds of an individual's convictions). And so the most that a man can do about the problem of evil is to convince himself that there are reasonable grounds for holding that a loving God can be responsible for all the evil and sin and suffering in the world. This I have tried briefly to do.

If the argument is sound, some vital conclusions flow from it. For if the possibility of responsible freedom provides the sole moral justification of the whole cosmic process of evolution, then freedom of choice and personal responsibility become more important for Christians than anything else in the world. If pain and suffering, evil and sin can only be justified in as much as they constitute the price worth paying for the emergence of beings capable of free response to God, then freedom of responsible choice is the most precious gift that men can receive. The worst sin of all will not be pride or envy or anger or avarice: it will be rather the dictatorship of the mind, or the domination of the will or the manipulation of the affections. Nothing can be more evil than these because they remove from others the possibility of responsible choice.

If men are to choose responsibly, they must learn to know what they are choosing. The aim of education must be to help young people to be clear, honest and open-minded in their thinking. They must be able to distinguish what is true from what is false or a half-truth. Advertisements blare, the television screen mesmerises, and newspapers persuade. The blandishments of the hidden persuaders tend to take away the exercise of responsible freedom of choice. If education can restore this freedom, it is furthering the purpose of God.

Another major cause of enslavement is the domination of a parent over his or her child. Mothers in particular tend to squeeze their offspring with the tentacles of smother-love. In so far as men can become more self-aware, they become capable of being freed from emotional enslavement and thus more able to make a free response to Divine Love. In so far as a man is able to become aware of his social conditioning, he also becomes capable of emancipation and so more able to make a free response to God.

All forms of totalitarianism, whether personal, political or ecclesiastical, are damnable because they frustrate the divine purpose underlying the kind of world in which we live. Attempts by groups to dominate decisions, or to dictate beliefs, are as evil as similar attempts by individuals. Equally evil is the attempt to impose a religious response which is automatic, unthinking and conditioned. Similarly the inculcation of a particular moral code of conduct by fear of physical punishment or spiritual penalty does more harm than good. It removes the capacity for free responsible choice, and thereby frustrates the purpose of the Creator.

Man who is free to make a response of his whole personality to his Creator has fulfilled the primary purpose for which he has been made. He is open to accept and to return the love of God. Yet how will he be able to recognise divine love? In the world of nature and men he sees distorted mirrors of divine charity, insufficient to give him full assurance of the nature of the divine activity which surrounds him. The Christian claim is that God, who by his activity in the natural world reveals his character, has given a special revelation of himself in a human person. If God's love is uniquely revealed in Jesus of Nazareth, man has a unique opportunity of responding to divine charity through the person of Jesus. To the person of Jesus we must next turn.

2. THE SINLESSNESS OF JESUS

We have tried to face honestly certain accusations against God. An attempt must now be made to face equally honestly some accusations against Jesus. I want to consider some of the grounds on which it has been alleged that Jesus, on certain occasions, failed to live up to his own teaching. There is however little point in such an investigation unless there are grounds for holding that Jesus could have made a perfect response to God. We shall therefore have to examine also the belief, so deeply embedded in the apostolic writings, that Jesus was sinless (He. 4.15; 2 Cor. 5.21; 1 Peter 2.22; 1 John 3.5; cf. John 8.46).

There is, however, a prior question to be raised, although by its nature no definite answer can be given to it. We may ask whether, if God was to be incarnate, it was necessary for him to have been capable of perfect response. At first sight this might seem positively undesirable. If God is to help sinners, must he not become a sinner himself? Is it enough that he should live among sinners? We may perhaps

grant that a man who has never succumbed
to temptation exposes himself continually to its
undiminished force, while a person who has
given way to temptation has found that its attractions, at least for a time, have been diminished.
And yet may not one who has never submitted
to temptation find that he has thereby strength-
ened himself against its attractions? Moreover,
he will never have known that kind of temptation
which is caused by past sin, especially when it
assails one whose will has been long weakened
by sinful habits. If God wants to help such
people, must he not "dirty his hands" and
descend to their level? Moreover, we know that
many undesirable traits of character are partly
inherited and partly the result of environment.
We know too that the years of childhood, especially the early years, can have lasting results
for good or ill on the human personality. If
God is to share our human condition, should he
not plumb its depths? Jesus of Nazareth did
indeed suffer terrible humiliation when crucified.
Yet he was born into a secure home. His mother
was a lower middle class teenage girl of pious
connections and good family. Joseph was a skilled
woodworker who does not seem to have lacked
employment. Would it not have been more congruous that God Incarnate should have been born
as the neglected child of a broken home into

a family of dissolute and depraved criminals, living in appalling conditions just above the level of starvation? Would there not then be hope for all mankind, even for the refuse of humanity?

Such an argument appeals to the heart more than to the head. Jesus before he died did experience temptation and anxiety, despair and dereliction. A man who shows true compassion must have experiential knowledge similar to that which calls forth his compassion, but he does not need himself to have been the subject of identical experience. In any case God is different from man. Since God's love holds all men in being, it reaches out to the most degenerate of men. To such a person the example of One who has won through to a perfect human response to God can be more inspiring than a mere descent by God Incarnate to the depths of human degradation where perfect human response would be impossible.

The human life of Jesus was not merely the example but also the instrument of divine love. In order that this instrument might be fully effective, a perfect response of human love was necessary. Arguing from a human perspective, it would seem that only the perfect response of human love could adequately mirror the divine charity, and only this perfect human response

could be the adequate instrument of God's reconciling love. In his death Jesus achieved this
perfect response, and such perfect human love
requires a secure background in which to be
nurtured. In Christian tradition Jesus' death
has been understood as the instrument of God's reconciling love. His death of course cannot be
separated from his life. His life led up to his
death. Yet Jesus' death has been the focus of
attention because it was the culmination and
consummation of his life. When he died his
obedience to his heavenly Father was perfectly
unified.

I do not think that the early Fathers bothered
themselves with the problem of Jesus' sinlessness.
They concentrated on the divinity of Jesus, and
they assumed that if he was divine, he must
have lived a unique and perfect life. According to
their teaching, the eternal Son of God indis-
solubly united to his godhead a complete human
nature. But he did not thereby become a human
person, since the eternal Son remained the subject
of the human nature which he had assumed. As
I have tried to explain elsewhere,[1] this way of
thinking about the person of Christ has become
difficult for many people to-day. If, however,

[1] " Towards a Christology for Today ", *Soundings*
(ed. A. R. Vidler, 1962).

it may be accepted that in the man Jesus the divine activity was fully operative so far as this is possible in human personality; if it may be held that the paradox of grace provides the best analogy whereby we may conceive of the union of the divine and human in Jesus; then it is possible, I think, to glimpse a further reason why it seems to us congruous with Incarnation that Jesus at his death should have made a perfect response to God. For grace does not destroy nature, but perfects it. If grace were to destroy nature, then the kind of human nature which Jesus assumed becomes comparatively irrelevant. But if grace perfects nature, only a full and complete human response to God could be perfected by grace to be an adequate instrument and example of the Divine Love. So it would seem, so far as human thinking is able or may dare to speculate on such matters.

Before we consider whether it is possible for a human man to be sinless, let us recall how we defined sin with reference to the problem of evil. Sin is a small word with many meanings. It is usually employed to signify some kind of sexual deviation; but this is far from its basic meaning. We said that at root sin is a state of estrangement from God, resulting in estrangement in our relationships with other people. The state of estrangement leads to sinful attitudes.

The worst of these have been held in Christian tradition to be Pride, Envy, Sloth, Intemperance, Avarice and Lust. I gave some reasons for holding that the worst sin of all is deliberately to deprive a person of his freedom of moral choice.

Many actions have evil effects or are wrong in themselves; but we cannot be held responsible for them unless they result from a deliberate act of will on the part of the agent to depart from what he knows to be right. A compulsive act, done in despite of the will, may be called a sin if we like to use the word, but it is not blameworthy. Many sins, of course, do not issue in actions at all, but are expressed in words, or remain locked up as attitudes or thoughts of the mind. It is not for any man to judge anyone guilty of sin, since no one can know the secret thoughts of another's heart; nor can he know the degree of responsible freedom that the other enjoys.

Original sin was believed to be '' the fault and corruption of the Nature of every man, that naturally is engendered in the offspring of Adam '' (Article IX). Some Fathers (notably Augustine) believed that all sexual intercourse was accompanied by some degree of *concupiscentia* or lust; and they held that it is fitting that children should be born in original sin inasmuch as they are the outcome of such sexual acts.

Jesus, however, was "incarnate by the Holy Ghost of the Virgin Mary". Since it was believed that human inheritance was derived from the male, Jesus was therefore considered to be free from this taint. He was "like unto us in all things, sin only except, in which he was clearly void, both in his flesh and in his spirit" (Article xv).

Modern knowledge of reproduction would seem to deny such a conclusion. For, when human conception takes place, twelve chromosomes of every zygote are derived from the mother. In the case of a virginal conception, at least some of the mother's chromosomes must be presumed to go to the making of the developing organism, or the child could not properly be called her own; and so the mother's inheritance would bear the same taint of original sin as the human father's would have done.

Our difficulty is evaded rather than avoided if the Papal Definition be accepted that Mary was immaculately conceived. For the question arises: how could Mary have possibly been born by normal human generation without the entail of her parents' inheritance? In Mary's case it is agreed that two human persons, not one, were concerned in her conception, so that miraculous freedom from original sin would be even more extraordinary in her case than in that of her Son. Moreover there is no scriptural or other primitive evidence for the belief in her immaculate conception; and Jesus' attitude towards his Mother, as portrayed in the Scriptures, would seem to me to provide evidence against rather than in favour of such a dogma.

The whole premise of the argument must, however, be denied. Adam and Eve did not exist, and so no taint could be inherited from them. Original sin is the result of man's evolutionary past which has affected his whole personality, his mind as well as his feelings and his body. As a result, original sin has affected the whole atmosphere of human society. We are born prone to sin, with a natural tendency to give free expression to animal appetites and passions, and conditioned by the society into which we are born. In consequence we have a tendency to self-interest and self-concern; and when this is frustrated we indulge in negative attitudes towards God, our neighbours and ourselves. These attitudes may either be openly expressed, or suppressed into unconsciousness.

If original sin comes from our evolutionary past, and affects the whole personality, then no human being can be without it. He cannot avoid his natural inheritance. If God was incarnate, then he must have been born in original sin, if the phrase is used with the meaning defined above. For if he had been born without these inborn tendencies, he would not have been a really human person.

It was because Jesus inherited original sin that he was tempted. These moral struggles were real struggles (cf. Mark 1. 13; 14.34f.). If these temptations were not real (i.e. if Jesus could not have voluntarily made the wrong decision), then he did not fully share our human nature.

It was precisely because the early Fathers were unwilling to allow that Jesus could have sinned that they were chary at first of ascribing to Jesus a human soul. For the human soul is by nature what they called *treptos*. It is fallible. It may be unstable. It can be dominated by the natural appetites and passions. It can fall a prey to corrupt imaginations. The Fathers tended to underemphasise Jesus' humanity. Even Apollinarius, the stalwart supporter of orthodoxy against Arianism, himself fell into heresy by denying to Jesus a human soul; for he feared that otherwise he would be detracting from the divinity of Christ and destroying the unity of his person. The early Church came to realise that Apollinarius was wrong. For if Jesus did not have a human soul, he could not help the rest of mankind who all have human souls. Nowadays we reject the " faculty psychology " which divides man up into body, soul and spirit. Nevertheless what the Fathers meant by the human soul is an integral aspect of human personality.

The early Fathers were interested in the childhood of Jesus in connection with his divinity. Somehow they had to combine in one Person both the impassible nature of godhead and the developing human nature of one who " as he grew up, advanced in wisdom and in favour with God and men " (Luke 2.52; cf. 1 Sam. 2.26). They were not interested in Jesus' childhood in so far as it concerned his sinlessness, for sinlessness was no problem for them.

For those of us, however, who believe that the foundations of human character are laid during the formative years of childhood, these early years of Jesus are of interest. A child is incapable of actual sins until it reaches the age of moral responsibility. It is impossible to determine this age with precision; and it differs with differing rates of individual development. Yet if a child is incapable of deliberate sins, he certainly acquires habits which lead to these by the time that he reaches an age when he is capable of moral freedom. Both inheritance and environment play a very large part in the development of a child's personality. We all know cases of very remarkable people who have emerged from appalling backgrounds. Nevertheless, if a grown person is to be capable of a *perfectly* unified response to God before he dies, he must be expected to have not only a remarkably fine genetical inheritance, but also a quite extraordinary upbringing. He must have enjoyed the security of exceptionally intelligent and unselfish love on the part of his mother. Protestants who deny a special supernatural status to Mary the Mother of God cannot reasonably withhold the highest human honours to her who bore and nurtured Jesus of Nazareth.

We know almost nothing about the childhood of Jesus. (The fantastic tales of the apocryphal gospels can be discounted. They were manufactured to meet a popular need.) Yet this may be said: it is at least possible, although it may well be profitless, to imagine Jesus' childhood. It need not have been dull. We rightly suspect that a Little Lord Fauntleroy is suppressing reactions that may later have dreadful results. High spirits, good-natured pranks and even occasional disobedience are not evidence of present imbalance or future sin. A four year old boy who takes a live beetle to pieces for the first time may be merely displaying an interest in the Creator's world. If he adds small pieces of red pottery to the family stew he may be trying to improve the appearance of the dish. If he ruins his father's handiwork by painting gaudy designs

on a newly carpentered object, he may be trying
to help, not hinder. If he disobeys his parents
when they give him without explanation what
seems an unreasonable order, he may be showing
sturdy common sense. There is no evidence to
suppose that the child Jesus did any of these
things; but, if he did, his behaviour could be
in keeping with one who, as a man, was to reach
human perfection.

Of Jesus' adolescence, only one instance is
recorded in the canonical gospels. When Jesus
was twelve, he broke away on one occasion
from the family group. His parents evidently
thought that he had treated them rather badly
(Luke 2.48). Would not a sinless son have warned
his parents that he was staying behind in Jeru-
salem and thus have saved them worry? We
cannot answer this question, for we do not know
the full circumstances. We do know, however,
that there comes a time in adolescence when a
boy must break away from his parents if he is to
call his soul his own. In the East this may
well happen earlier rather than later. Jesus was
later to emphasise the priority of God's claims
over those of the family. At this time his life
was centred on God (Luke 2.49), and with over-
fond parents it may have been kinder to be
stern. We do not know. In any case a thought-
less action is not necessarily a sinful one. The

incident is not incompatible with one who was to reach human perfection.

From the age of twelve until his baptism the life of Jesus is unknown to us. Any inference about these '' hidden years '' must be an argument from silence. It seems, however, that when Jesus returned during his public ministry to his home-town, the townsfolk were astonished at his wisdom and at his spiritual authority (Mark 6.1ff.; John 6.42). They found his present role inappropriate to his earlier character and to his family connections. This incident suggests not that Jesus' earlier years were marked by sin, but that they were uneventful. There is no reason to doubt that he had lived quietly as a faithful and observant Jew. It suggests that others who also live quiet and uneventful lives may be making an appropriate response to life. It also suggests that Jesus' life had not, before his baptism, reached its full human potentialities. It suggests that his response to God was not yet fully unified.

Jesus' experience at his baptism, so far as it can be recovered from the gospel records, seems in many respects akin to the psychological effects of a sudden conversion. There was a sudden and intense personal experience of God. There was a new awareness of personal status with God, a call to a new way of life and the acceptance of that call. There was, in fact, a re-orientation

of his whole human personality. Unlike most
religious conversions of the " twice-born " type,
there seems to have been no awareness of sin; and
this suggests that Jesus was not conscious of
having sinned, even in his " hidden years ".
The question arises in this connection why Jesus
was baptised. I have suggested elsewhere[2] that the
Baptist preached a baptism not of repentance
(as in Mark 1.4) but of ritual washing (as in
Josephus, *Antiqu.* 18.5.2). But if Mark is right,
and John did preach a baptism of repentance,
Jesus could hardly have been baptised unless he
had some sense of sin. (It is difficult to see how
he would have consciously offered a vicarious
repentance before his ministry had begun. It is
equally difficult to see how he could have offered
himself for a baptism of repentance without having
any feelings of guilt.) These guilt feeling could
have been the result of his upbringing. They
would not prove that Jesus had sinned against
his heavenly Father; they would only suggest that
he felt that he had done so.

After this baptism experience, elements of Jesus'
human personality which had been suppressed,
or which had previously existed only in poten-
tiality, were united into a new synthesis. This is
not, of course, to deny in any way that this bap-
tismal experience was a genuine experience by

Jesus of his heavenly Father. His psychological
processes would not have been different in kind
from our own. If God's grace is mediated through
a psychological experience of conversion (and I
know from experience that this can be so), then
in Jesus' case did not the divine activity work
through Jesus' psychological experience at his
baptism? After all, if Jesus was a real human
being, the development of his human personality
must have been similar in kind to that of other
men. His conscience must have been formed like
our consciences. His human will must have oper-
ated in the same mode as our human wills operate.
His religious convictions must have been formed
in the same kind of way as ours have been formed.
"He that sanctifies and they that are sanctified
are all of one: for which cause he is not ashamed
to call them brethren" (He. 2.11).

To say that Jesus was without sin is not the
same as to say that he was always humanly perfect. Whatever else it may mean, Jesus' reply
in Mark 10.18: "Why do you call me good?
There is none good, except one, God" suggests
an awareness of human limitations. It is human
to develop. A man must progress or regress.
Not to change is either subhuman (in the sense
of retarded development) or superhuman (in the
sense of transcendence of human limitations). The

gospel records suggest a theological development during the short period of Jesus' ministry (for such a development contrast Mark 9.1, Matt. 10.23, and Mark 13.32). The impossibility of making a coherent synthesis of all Jesus' teaching suggests not merely some inaccuracies and alterations in the words attributed to him, but also a development of thought in his own mind. This in turn suggests, if we may speak with reverence and reserve, a psychological development. Professor Grensted has written of "a full and complete turning to God, from the Baptism", and yet of a process "in which there is progressive unification".[3] He noted that at Jesus' temptation on the occasion of his Baptism, the Spirit and the Devil appear as opposing forces. At his Transfiguration "the Cross is represented not by Satan but by the friendly figures of Moses and Elijah"; while at Gethsemane the forces which dominate his life are no longer personified, but "merged in the final surrender".[4] This does not mean that Jesus was a sinful person who became progressively less sinful and more obedient to God's will.

[3] Appendix on "The Sinlessness of Jesus" in *The Person of Christ* (1933), p. 279.

[4] Professor Grensted also sees significance in that Jesus' warfare against the demons is confined to the early part of his ministry.

For he conquered *all* his temptations: he was never disobedient to his heavenly Father. The evidence does, however, suggest that it was not until Jesus' final temptation that his human personality was completely unified. At each stage he made the fullest and most complete response to his Father of which he was capable at the time, a response which always issued in obedience. This is what we mean when we say that he conquered all his temptations. The Epistle to the Hebrews asserts that Jesus " was tempted in all respects as we are, yet without sin " (4.15). Yet this does not contradict the further assertion that " although he was Son, yet he learnt obedience from what he suffered, and was made perfect " (5.8f.). The author did not mean that Jesus learnt how to obey through these sufferings, nor that he learnt obedience as one who had not known it before. Rather he took obedience up to the point of death, to the point beyond which it could not be taken. The greater the test, the profounder the obedience it evoked. If we may dare to speak of such things, the progressive unification of the Incarnate Son's human personality reached its perfection at his death. In this situation of ultimate concern, when he was under the pressure of emotional shock and physical distress, he was able to give the full and per-

fect obedience of his whole personality. The
tradition suggests that throughout his life he
was sinless and that at his death he reached
absolute human perfection. There was no greater
test possible. It is fruitless to ask what would
have happened had he been brain-washed with
the full Pavlovian treatment. He could not,
under such conditions, have learnt fuller obedience, since he would have been less able to
make a *voluntary* submission to his Father's
will.

It is not impossible for a human person to
make this full and complete turning to God.
Jesus had good genetic inheritance. He was born
of a good family, into a secure home, with a
loving Mother. He was born of a race which
had a unique insight into the relationship of
God and man. He was born at a time when the
Jews were perhaps more concerned with their
religion than at any other time. In other words,
the Incarnate Lord was born at what Christians
believe was "the fullness of time".

He had too the stimulus of an emotional shock,
provided by John's teaching and baptism, to
unify his personality and to draw out its potentialities. Such a stimulus was required for progressive unification. The final challenge of Jesus'
arrest, trial and passion provided the ultimate
challenge through which humanly speaking, he

achieved a fully unified response of obedience to his Father. In these things the grace of God was operative throughout.

But any man who turns to God, however fully, is inevitably subject to the limiting conditions of humanity and to the conditioning factors of his environment. There is unavoidable ignorance imposed by human limitations of knowledge. There are the ambiguities of all human decisions, from which evil as well as good inevitably results. There are contemporary beliefs (such as the first century belief in Adam as the primal man) which later generations would repudiate.

These limiting factors common to humanity conditioned Jesus' response to his Father; yet at his Passion he achieved this perfectly unified response of obedience to his Father. This perfection should not daunt those who know their calling to imitate Jesus but who know too their imperfection and frailty. God calls all men to obedience; and part of that obedience is the acceptance of our inability to make a perfectly unified response. God does not ask us for more than we can give him.

In the light of this discussion, some particular accusation against Jesus' personal sinlessness may be considered.[5] They must be measured against his own standards, for there are none higher.

Many of these objections rest on a misunderstanding of Jesus' teaching. Thus the parables of Jesus do not give examples of ethical behaviour: they are used to show, in graphic form, the implications of Jesus' messianic role, and to confront men with decisions about it. The Parable of the Unjust Steward (Luke 16.1ff.) is concerned not with the ethics of stewardship, but with the necessity of resolute action in a crisis. The Parable of the Labourers in the Vineyard (Matt. 20.1-16) is not about social justice, but it is a vindication of Christ's friendships with and care for religious outcasts. The Parable of the Marriage Feast (Luke 14. 7ff.) is meant to teach humility for its own sake, not the material advantages which accrue from a humble attitude. The Parable of the Treasure in a Field is intended to confront readers with the overriding claims of the Kingdom of God, and not to suggest a method of buying real estate for less than its potential value (Matt. 13.44).

Other objections to Jesus' teaching rest on a misunderstanding of semitic modes of expression. Thus Jesus' words recorded in Mark 3.33ff., or

[5] I am much indebted to Dr. Hastings Rashdall's list of objections to Jesus' moral teaching in *Christ and Conscience* (1916), pp. 164-94.

Luke 14.26, or Matt. 8.22 (=Luke 9.60) are not intended to depreciate the family. They are vivid expressions used to show that the demand of the Kingdom has priority over the claims of the home. " Let the dead bury the dead " is not a hard-hearted expression: it means that the need for preaching the Kingdom is more urgent than Jewish funeral rites. Similarly the words " take no thought for the morrow " (Matt. 6.34) are not meant as a warning against the cardinal virtue of prudence. They are a warning against excessive worry about material possessions. Again, Jesus' teaching about rewards and punishment is not prudential. " Jesus offers rewards to those who follow him without hope of reward " (Bultmann).

It is never possible to say with absolute certainty what Jesus actually said, to what extent his words have been altered by early tradition, and what liberty the evangelists took with their sources. Many have thought that the words of Matt. 7.6 show the marks of later tradition: " Give not that which is holy to the dogs, nor cast your pearls before swine . . ." It has been objected that these words show contempt for people and thus fall below the standards which Jesus himself set. In fact they give good advice, cast into proverbial form.

A similar objection could be brought against Jesus' words to the Syro-Phoenician woman (Mark 7.27; Matt. 15.26). Was he not harsh in speaking of Gentiles as "dogs"? Should not he have given the same loving attention to the woman in her distress as he gave to his fellow-Jews? This objection raises the whole question of Jesus' messianic vocation. He believed, on the basis of biblical teaching, and the guidance of the Holy Spirit, that he was only sent to the lost sheep of the house of Israel (Matt. 15. 24; cf. 10.6). The ingathering of the Gentiles into God's kingdom was, according to Jewish tradition, reserved for the Last Days. Jesus seems to have accepted this teaching inasmuch as he never himself took active steps to help Gentiles, although he never finally repulsed any that came to him. He even spoke to one in the most commendatory terms (Matt. 8.10; Luke 7.9). If Jesus was mistaken about his messianic role, this objection has force. Those who believe that he was not mistaken find that this objection against Jesus' sinlessness melts away when it is seen against the background of his vocation.

There are occasions when Jesus is accused of showing petulance, anger and loss of temper. The cursing of the fig-tree is a case in point (Mark 11.13; cf. Matt. 21.19). It is said that

Jesus behaved irresponsibly. Many scholars have
thought that the incident as recorded in Mark
or Matthew is unhistorical, and that it is derived
from the Parable of the Fig-Tree (Luke 21.29ff.).
But even if the incident is historical, Jesus cannot
properly be called petulant. According to pro-
phetic tradition, " acted parables " can be used
to signify God's judgement, as well as to help
in some measure to bring this judgement to
pass. The cursing of the fig-tree must be seen
as an acted parable of the rejection of Israel, con-
sequent on Israel's rejection of her Messiah.

Jesus is reported to have shown anger when
healing a man with a withered hand (Mark 3.5).
He was angry because the onlookers, instead of
rejoicing that a man should be made whole, were
watching for evidence to bring against him for
breaking the Sabbath tradition. If anger is in-
consistent with love, Jesus certainly lapsed from
his own standard. But anger is sometimes the
very expression of love. Perhaps the best illustration of this is from family life. A child will
tell you that it much prefers its mother to be
angry on occasions when it has created a nuisance.
Sweet reasonableness usually hides suppressed
resentment. Reaction to frustration when it affects
someone else is righteous anger. This is part of
human nature. Reaction to frustration when it
affects *ourselves* is a different matter altogether,

but it is irrelevant to the scriptural passage under consideration.

These considerations apply also to Jesus' cleansing of the Temple. He was not angry because of a personal slight to himself. He was furious because the Court of the Gentiles was cluttered up with men who made money from religion. People were not able to use the Court for the purpose for which it was made, and the truths of the Jewish religion were being horribly obscured. Had Jesus contained and suppressed his anger, then we might well doubt his sinlessness. He gave it violent expression in a fully human reaction. Neither Jesus nor the Christian Church condemn the use of every kind of violence. Violence is not *ipso facto* a sin, any more than anger is sinful unless it is anger " without cause " (Matt. 5.22), i.e., unjustified rage.

I have left to the end what seem to me the two major objections against the sinlessness of Christ. The first is arrogance. Let me first say that I would agree that the Christ of the Fourth Gospel is arrogant; but I do not believe that the Christ of the Fourth Gospel speaks the words of Jesus of Nazareth. The life and teaching of Jesus have passed through the crucible of its author's mind, and the worsening relationship of Christians and Jews at the time when it was written has left its mark upon the monologues

of Jesus, and especially on his dialogues with
the Jews. I suppose that the words of the
Fourth Gospel have played a large part in estab-
lishing the doctrine of Jesus' sinlessness. "Which
of you convinceth me of sin?" we read (John
8.46). These words testify to the author's convictions rather than to the evidence on which
he rested them. It is true that the dialogues of the
Fourth Gospel are Jewish in tone, and that a
distinguished Jewish critic has called this gospel
the most Jewish of the four. But this only sheds
light on the background of the author.

Does Jesus show the same arrogance in the
synoptic gospels? "Come unto me, all that
labour and are heavy laden" (Matt. 11.28) has
been said to express self-importance. There are
other texts which could similarly be cited. Jesus
did not dare to understate his role (how could
he, if his claims were true?) but he attracted
people to himself in order to bring them to God,
and not to dominate them with his own human
personality.

The last objection is the weightiest. I would
like to put it forward in the words of my Jewish
cousin, the late Dr. Claude Montefiore, for whom
I have a profound respect. Anything he wrote,
I think, is worth reading. In this connection he
said: "What one would have wished to find
would be one single incident in which Jesus

actually performed one loving deed to one of his Rabbinic antagonists or enemies.''[6] An ounce of practice, he wrote, would be worth a ton of theory. I think that, so far as the Gospel evidence goes, his complaint is almost justified. There are however hints of a happier relationship between Jesus and the Pharisees than that which the gospels generally portray. For example, Jesus once commended a Scribe (Mark 12.34). Again, the Pharisees who warned Jesus to flee from Herod (Luke 13.31) presumably liked him. On another occasion Jesus was eating in the house of a Pharisee (Luke 7.36). This suggests that Jesus was at least on terms of friendship with Pharisees. We have to admit, however, that the wholesale condemnation of the Pharisees which is found in the Gospels (especially in Matt. 23) is unfair. We are not concerned to prove that during his ministry Jesus' fully human response was always perfectly unified. If Jesus spoke all these words, he might have been justified in the case of particular Pharisees, but would have done less than justice to Pharisees as a whole. Unfortunately these particular sayings of Jesus have been edited by an anti-Pharisaic author, just as the selection of incidents and sayings in the Gospels as a whole is dependent upon and sub-

[6] C. G. Montefiore, *Rabbinic Literature and Gospel Teaching* (1930), p.104.

ject to alteration by the interests of the Evangelists.

We can hardly, however, take exception at attack as such. Attack is, at times, the most loving way of bringing people to the truth. Similarly we must not object to Jesus' warnings about the future consequences of present attitudes. If his teaching on this subject is true, it would have been unloving to withhold it. Mr. E. M. Forster has written that it is because of such warnings that he would prefer not to meet Jesus of Nazareth if he had the chance. Mr. Forster is a much loved and much respected Humanist who is all for a peaceful life in which everyone is kind to one another. God forbid that I should depreciate kindness; yet I think the real reasons why Mr. Forster would prefer not to meet Jesus if he could are, firstly, the terrible things that people have done in Jesus' name, and secondly, Mr. Forster's disbelief in the burden of the preaching and teaching of Jesus.

I have tried to mention some of the objections to Jesus as a sinless man. I doubt if what I have said would satisfy a non-believer; for the arguments that I have used are necessarily arguments from silence or arguments of interpretation. They are compatible with the belief that Jesus achieved human perfection but they do not compel that belief.

What does? I suppose in the last resort it is the impact of the Man who bursts through the records of the Gospels. One must acknowledge that the Evangelists were as biased in favour of Jesus' sinlessness as the writers of the Epistles. It is uncommon to be critical of a hero: it is even more improbable if you happen to believe that this hero was God Incarnate. The Gospels show some signs that details were removed which might have been thought to contain criticism of Jesus by his disciples, and that words of Jesus were altered which might have been regarded as self-depreciating. Matthew has been more careful than Mark; and John even more careful than Matthew. No doubt the Old Testament analogy of the Paschal Lamb without blemish, and the Old Testament prophecy of the Suffering Servant who " had done no violence, nor was deceit found in his mouth " had some influence on the writers. Nevertheless it is not the literary creation of an evangelist, but the portrait of a living Person who meets me in the gospel pages. The self-awareness that is a by-product of sanctity leads all the Saints to admit their unworthiness. But this Person seems without any consciousness of sin. I see no reason to modify some words which I have written in another connection:

There can be no advance beyond Jesus in strength of will, intuitive knowledge of God

and man, love of neighbour, relationship
with our Heavenly Father—in fact, in moral
and spiritual perfection of character as we
know it.[7]

This is not just my own experience. It is
the corporate expression of the Christian Church
down the ages, and the individual experience
of all believing Christians. What is more, the
perfection of Jesus has not left them merely
with the inspiring example of a good man. It
has also brought home to them conviction of
their own imperfection. If I may quote again
from what I have written elsewhere: "Look at
the Figure who towers over everyone else. Can
you judge him? Do you not find, in the act
of judging him, that he judges you?"[8]

I have spoken of the sinlessness of Jesus of
Nazareth. I have been concerned with him simply
as a human person. Perhaps it is at this point,
where he judges us, which leads us from admira-
tion of his human perfection to the conviction (to
use biblical language) that he is our Saviour.
"God was in Christ reconciling the world to
himself." To this theme we must now turn.

[7] *Soundings*, p. 150.
[8] *Beyond Reasonable Doubt*, p. 25.

3. ATONEMENT AND PERSONALITY

In this third lecture I shall examine the great theme of Atonement through Christ. It is a commonplace that there is in Christendom no ecumenical definition of this doctrine, such as exists, for example, in the case of the Person of Christ. Various churches and confessions and fellowships may have their own dogma of the Atonement, but there is no single statement of doctrine which is representative of all Christendom on this subject. Moreover, there is no single New Testament doctrine. There are some particular statements, notably in the writings of St. Paul, which have later been made the foundation of whole systems of dogma, but there is in the New Testament no single doctrine. In the post-war years theologians, under the influence of so-called biblical theology, have been at pains to emphasise—and to over-emphasise—the unity of the Bible. There is indeed in the Bible a remarkable unity of direction. All the books of the New Testament are written in the Church for the Church by members of the Church in order to witness to the impact of the advent of Christ on the lives of the writers and on the life of the

Church. But within this primary unity there is evident pluralism. For example the four Gospels all write from different viewpoints and therefore contain rather different doctrines of Christ. The author of the Epistle to the Hebrews, while he has a lot in common with St. Paul, writes from a viewpoint different from his. Even St. Paul is not always consistent; the contents of his later Epistles cannot always be reconciled with his earlier writings.

The doctrine of Atonement must be examined within the context of this pluralist theology. Even the very word Atonement is not a New Testament word. It is a kind of theological umbrella which covers all the New Testament expressions of the way in which the life, death and resurrection of Christ affects the relations of men with God.

We have to take seriously the fact of the canon of Scripture. Usually the canon is emphasised so as to promote uniformity of doctrine. "You must keep to the biblical doctrine", we are told, "that is why the Church formed its canon of scripture." In fact the true effect of the canon should be not to promote uniformity, but to permit theological plurality. Consider 1 Tim. 3-16, where the event of Christ is described not as an atonement for sin but as a revelation which gives meaning to life:

He was manifested in the flesh
vindicated in the Spirit
  seen by angels,
preached among the nations,
believed on in the world,
  taken up in glory.

Consider next the Epistle of St. James. It would be hard to say that this Epistle has any doctrine at all of Atonement through the work of Christ. Indeed, Christ is only mentioned twice in the whole letter (1.1; 2.1). The reader is certainly admonished: "Draw near to God, and he will draw near to you" (4.8). Yet there is no suggestion here that since the coming of Christ it has been possible for Christians to draw near to God, and that this was something which formerly was impossible. In this Epistle sin and death as well as temptation seem equally real possibilities for Christians as for non-Christians (1.13f.). I am not commending this viewpoint of the author of St. James' Epistle. I am only concerned to point out that it is to be found within the New Testament. To condemn a book of the New Testament as unchristian is to form a canon within the canon. It suggests that we are wiser than our fathers. The early Church did not include a book in the canon simply because of a belief that it had an apostolic author. Part of the proof of its apostolicity was to be seen in the apostolic nature of its contents. So, then, the early Church must have regarded the theology of the Epistle of St. James as a perfectly legitimate expression of Christian thought. The fact that this Epistle has no Christian doctrine of the Atonement is not a reason for discarding it from the canon. The plurality of theologies in the canon of Scripture should awaken us to the need to accept a plurality of legitimate doctrine as well as to the danger of defining one single formula as the adequate expression of a particular Christian dogma.

In so far as any generalisation is possible, it is fair to say that the New Testament as a whole proclaims a new relationship for man with God through the event of Jesus Christ. The authors of the New Testament writings speak out of an experience which they have shared with their fellow-members of the Church. They seek to put this experience into words. They use images and concepts which come to hand. Inasmuch as the Christian Church saw itself as the Israel of God, the most obvious images and concepts lay to hand in the Old Testament scriptures. The New Testament authors also chose images and concepts which fitted both their frame of thought and their individual temperaments. Thus the author of the Epistle to the Hebrews, who had been brought up as a Jew and who knew intimately the details of the Jewish sacrificial cultus, naturally described the work of Jesus in terms of sacrifice. This was an image and a concept derived from the Old Testament, and it suited the author's particular interests and temperament. Again, Paul, who had been brought up at Gamaliel's feet and instructed in Rabbinic law, naturally tended to think of the work of Christ primarily in terms of justification, an idea which also had an Old Testament background. The author of the Johannine literature, on the other hand, although he was reacting against a gnostic interpretation of Christianity, yet instinctively used gnostic categories of thought; and thus for him the work of Christ is understood rather as light shining out in the prevailing darkness, truth over against opposing falsehood, eternal spirit against earthly mortality.

The mode by which Christians are caught up into the new reality inaugurated by Christ is differently described by different writers and variously described by each particular author. Forgiving, healing, rescuing, sealing a pledge, justifying, consecrating, electing, redeeming, atoning, expiating, reconciling, incorporating into Christ, transforming the personality, bringing life or rebirth, recreating, overcoming the world, illuminating, bestowing the spirit of God and promising the glory of God—these are all different

images and concepts used to communicate both
the experience of the new reality and the mode of
its bestowal on men. Even this list is not exhaustive. Certainly no one of these images and
concepts is sufficient to communicate the richness
of the gift; and different images will appeal
differently to various people. It may be noted that
although some of these concepts seem to be indi-
vidualistic in their application, the authors of the
New Testament books took it for granted that the
locus of the new reality into which Christians
were caught up was the Christian Church.

The two New Testament works which come
nearest to containing a systematic doctrine of the
Atonement are the Epistles to the Romans and to
the Hebrews. The former contains a sustained
argument about justification. Closer examination
of the argument, however, shows that Paul's
exposition of justification is not properly a legal
argument at all. God's justification of men by
Christ, which men appropriate through faith, is
not a judge's sentence of acquittal, but the loving
welcome of a Heavenly Father who invites his
estranged children to live with him in his house
for ever. Although Paul uses legal terminology
he transcends juridicism. To pass from the
Epistle to the Romans to the Epistle to the
Hebrews, it will be seen that in the latter the
concept of sacrifice is treated in a similar kind

of way. Christ is not only the substance of the
sacrifice but also the officiating High Priest.
The imagery of immolation and the sprinkling
of blood is strained to the uttermost, since the
immolation of the one true sacrifice takes place
on Calvary, and the blood of the sacrifice is
offered there, but the sacrificial victim ever lives
to make intercession in heaven, which is described as the true tabernacle not made with hands.
The concept of levitical sacrifice is used in order
to interpret and to explain the efficacy and suffi-
ciency of the true sacrifice of Christ, but in so
doing the author turns upside down and inside
out the concept of sacrifice, as this was understood in the levitical ordinances. Neither Romans
nor Hebrews contains a systematic exposition
of the doctrine of the Atonement. Both moreover
take for granted unquestioned assumptions which
might well be questioned to-day. For Paul it is a
datum (derived from his own experience) that
from law comes knowledge of sin, and therefore Paul has to show that God's gift of gracious
forgiveness comes apart from law. But it may
be questioned whether Paul's personal experience
can properly be universalised in this way. Or
again, it is a datum for the author of the Epistle
to the Hebrews that without the shedding of blood
there can be no remission of sins. This datum
was no doubt derived from the sacrificial cultus;

but it is a doubtful generalisation for us to accept now that the sacrificial cultus has passed away.

Almost all of the images used in the New Testament are rooted in the experience of the writer, and many are found in the Old Testament. In the course of history the images which Paul used have, by and large, become normative for the Church. In speaking of *justification*, Paul communicated the feeling of vindication and release which an accused man experiences when he is acquitted; and the imagery emphasises, too, the sovereignty of God. In speaking of man's *redemption*, Paul communicated something of the cost of Christ's work, and the experience of freedom that manumission gave to a slave. The image also stresses the objective fact of Christ's redeeming work. By using the imagery of *sacrifice*, the very diversity of sacrificial types to which Paul alluded shows that he had no systematic presentation of Christ's death in sacrificial terms. Once again the objective fact of Christ's costly death is emphasised and the imagery communicates the feeling of expiation that the sacrificial cultus must have mediated. The imagery of *reconciliation* is found very seldom in Paul. It perhaps receives undue emphasis in Pauline exposition because it is one of his few images that is still alive to-day. It is appropriate inasmuch as it emphasises the restoration of a two-sidedly

personal relationship between God and man, but
it fails inasmuch as it suggests that man's relationship to God is the same as that towards
his fellow-men.

Not only does Paul use a great variety of
imagery to describe the effect of Christ on man's
relationship to God (and the list commented on
above is by no means exhaustive) but there are
also more far-reaching differences of doctrine
in the Pauline letters. At times Paul spoke of
a cosmic redemption (2 Cor. 5.19) and at other
times he wrote as though Christ became a human
being so as to save mankind (Ro. 8.3). Furthermore, Paul sometimes wrote so as to emphasise
the universal effect of Christ's death on all
mankind (Ro. 5.15; 1 Cor. 15.22); but elsewhere
he insisted on the necessity of faith as though
the effect of Christ's death was beneficial only
for those who accepted it (Ro. 5.1). It would
perhaps be fair to say that Paul believed that
Christ's death would have universal and indeed
cosmic effects, but that the benefits of his Passion
were only realised as yet among those who
accepted them in faith.

Paul regarded the death of Christ as the essence
of man's atonement with God. The Fourth Evangelist, for all his stress on the light of Christ
during his lifetime (cf. John 12.35) also regarded
Jesus' death as the main attractive power of his

redeeming love (John 12.32; cf. 10.11). By
contrast, in the Acts of the Apostles, it is Jesus'
resurrection that is highlighted, because it shows
the efficacy of his death (Acts 2.24). In St. Luke's
Gospel the Ascension is seen as the climax of
Christ's work (Luke 24.50f.). In Ephesians the
emphasis is rather on the gifts of the Spirit
poured out on those who have ascended with
Christ into the heavens. In the Book of Revelation the stress is on the final vindication of
Christ at the end of the age. Different writers
stress different aspects of the one work of Christ.
It is the whole work of Christ that may be properly called the work of Atonement.

In the history of doctrine, the Church has on
the whole followed St. Paul in putting primary
emphasis on the death of Christ (except perhaps
for the patristic period when men were preoccupied with definitions of Christology). Each
generation has had to interpret the biblical doctrine anew. The interpretation of Christ's atoning work in the bible was itself influenced by
the cultural, religious and pseudo-scientific
assumptions of the biblical period. The matter
of faith can never be purely abstracted from the
forms in which it is expressed. The total environment in which the New Testament was written
could never entirely reproduce itself later. Yet it
did not and has not absolutely changed, even

when man has " come of age ". Certain aspects
of the biblical interpretation still continued (and
continue) to "ring a bell" in the mind of the
readers without their having to make an act of
historical imagination such as is possible only
to a trained mind.

So far as the doctrine of the Atonement is concerned, the selection of particular "relevant"
passages from the bible has usually meant a
fragmentation of the total biblical picture of
God's atoning love. Certain sentences and phrases
have been abstracted, because they have seemed
particularly "relevant" to one generation, and
they have been made the foundation of a whole
systematisation of the doctrine such as a biblical
author never himself intended. To give a few
examples, Paul's remarks on justification have
become the foundation of juridical systems of
atonement; words of Jesus about his death " as
a ransom for many " have been the springboard
from which Jesus' death has been interpreted
as a ransom to the Devil; a passing reference
by Paul to the reconciliation effected by Christ's
death has given rise to whole theories about the
death of Christ as restoring the two-sidedly personal relationship between God and man; while
another remark about the constraint of God's
love in Christ has given birth to the so-called
Moral Influence theory of Atonement. Paul's

allusive statements that Christ was made sin for us, and that he became a curse for us, have produced theories of substitutionary punishment. Further instances could be multiplied.

Naturally the Christian faith has clothed itself in the thought-forms of the period in which it has been reformulated. A theory of the Atonement must be regarded in the light of the age in which it was formulated. To quote Professor Richardson:

Each has clothed itself with ideas of the type of society of its own period. Thus, the Ransom theory suggested by Origen was favoured by theologians throughout the period in which men's minds were dominated by the view of "rights" (including the "rights" of the Devil) upheld by Roman law; St. Anselm's Satisfaction theory was thereafter prevalent in the Middle Ages, when social thinking expressed itself in terms of the honour or satisfaction that should be rendered to one's overlord in feudal society; in the Reformation period, when forensic ideas of sin as the transgression of law were dominant, the various Penal theories were put forward; and finally Moral Influence theories of the Atonement were congenial to an age of toleration and universal suffrage, when persuasion and education had taken

the place of compulsion and dictation as
ideals of society.[1]

The task of each age is to hear with sufficient
distinctness the essence of the total biblical view
of Atonement, and to translate this into its own
thought-forms. To the extent that each generation
faithfully accomplished this, their translation
of the doctrine was valid. It was valid for
them; not necessarily for us. For what was a
valid translation for one age and culture may
be either meaningless or misleading to another.

Thus Origen's "Ransom theory" would be
largely meaningless to a generation which has
by and large lost its belief in the Devil; while
the mediaeval "Satisfaction theory" might well
be badly misleading to those who do not share
either the psychological or the sociological assumptions that formed the background of the theory.

At times this "translation" has resulted in
the formulation of a theory which actually con-
tradicts the biblical form of the doctrine. The
Reformation, founded on the Word of God in
the Bible, produced a theory of the Atonement
that was itself unbiblical! The marks of this
doctrine are still found in the Consecration
Prayer of the Book of Common Prayer where
there is commemorated "a full perfect and sufficient Sacrifice, Oblation and Satisfaction for the

[1] A. Richardson, *Christian Apologetics* (1947), p. 82f.

sins of the whole world ". Satisfaction is not only unbiblical but contradictory to biblical categories. It implies that the angry Father was appeased by the sacrifice of his loving and obedient Son. Scripture, on the other hand, attests that God sent his Son not to appease his wrath but to manifest his love. The Son did not, in the words of Article II, " reconcile his Father to us ". On the contrary God was in Christ reconciling the world to himself. This is a case where literary criticism has made a great contribution; for whereas in the past it was believed that *hilassesthai* could mean to appease (and hence to satisfy), recent research has shown that the Septuagintal use of the word signifies not appeasement but expiation (cf. C. H. Dodd, *The Bible and the Greeks* (1933), p. 93).

The situation to-day is very different from that of previous ages. This is chiefly due to the revolutionary effects both of technology on our lives and of the natural and social sciences on our ways of thought. For a few who have been nurtured in the life and language of the Church the old images continue to have power and meaning, for these images have not wholly lost touch with human experience. But for the great mass of people outside the Church, as well as for many within it, they lack meaning and power.

It is unlikely that any explanation of the Atonement will carry widespread conviction to-day that does not use accepted psychological categories. No image of the Atonement is likely to have meaning and power for many unless it is taken from a psychological model. For the doctrine of Atonement is concerned with the relationship of God and men. Matters of relationship concern fundamental human attitudes; and attitudes are the concern of psychology.

I have tried to explain elsewhere how the stresses and strains of life often force men back to childhood states without their realising that this has happened. The calamities of daily existence cause men to react unconsciously as well as consciously in order to protect themselves. As a result of unconscious regression men are often in a state of internal disharmony, and out of relationship with their family, friends and acquaintances. I wrote:

This regression to infantile behaviour may be classified into three main types, although individuals will not usually fit into any one category. Infantile rage may have caused compulsive attention-seeking behaviour, or it may have been inverted into mordant

despair, or it may have resulted in detach-
ment and distrust of social involvement and
personal relationships. This suppressed rage,
which in infancy was directed against the
mother-figure, becomes directed against the
self, or against all those with a claim on
man's affections, and especially against God,
the author and source of man's affections.[2]

This is of course a very oversimplified statement of the reasons for ineradicable psychological imbalance, for this may have many
causes, physical or psychological. Yet it may
be that here is the root of those apparently incurable spiritual sicknesses which are not severe
enough to be classed as madness but which cause
gross failure of personal relationships and which
express themselves by what theologians have
traditionally called the "deadly sins".

Whatever be the psychological causes, it remains true that most human beings unconsciously
reject themselves and unconsciously reject God.
In the first chapter, on the problem of evil, an
attempt was made to show that there are rational
grounds, as well as emotional causes, for man's
rejection of God's love. The death of Jesus can
be Atonement precisely because it manifests God
involving himself in human calamity and identi-
fying himself with men in their desperate plight.

[2] *Soundings* (ed. A. R. Vidler, 1962), p. 168f.

The story of the Cross is a story of injustice
and malice, betrayal and beating, denial and
despair, forsakenness and desolation, jealousy and
envy, spite and rage, taunting and mockery, rejection and condemnation. The Incarnate Son
suffered both as subject and as object. As subject, he underwent the crushing experience of
physical and psychic agony. As object, he
was the victim of his enemies' rage, his
acquaintances' indifference, and his friends'
weakness. God Incarnate endured the effects
of both the impersonal regularities which
govern human existence and the personal
assaults upon his human dignity inflicted by
friend and foe alike. God Incarnate suffered
to the full the evils of the world for which
God alone is ultimately responsible. He endured the impersonal cruelty of creation (no
miracle prevented his physical agony) and the
personal cruelty of malice and weakness (doctors
suggest that the reason why Jesus remained
alive for so short a time upon the Cross was the
emotional shock caused by the events of his
trial and thereafter). God subjected himself in
Christ to the impersonal cruelty of his own
physical world and to the personal cruelty of
malice and weakness inflicted by his own
creatures. ''Sometimes it is hard not to say
' God forgive God '. Sometimes it is hard to say

so much. But if our faith is true, He didn't. He crucified Him.''[3]

Here, and for me here alone, is the proof presented to faith that God is really love. It is only presented to *faith*. Man has, of course, the option of rejecting belief in God, or he may, if he wishes, reject the love of God whose existence he accepts. A man is never compelled to accept his acceptance at God's hands. Real sin consists in a deliberate refusal to accept his acceptance by God. For the death of Jesus removes the legitimate emotional and intellectual barriers to such belief.

Man can, then, no longer accuse God of being more like a devil than a loving Creator. He can no longer with justice charge God with creating a universe in which he is indifferent to its inevitable sin and suffering, evil and disaster. The death of Jesus shows God caring to the point at which he can care no more; that is, by sharing human pain to the point of human death. The death of Jesus shows God Incarnate accepting men even as they inflict upon him the worst that they can do. He seems even to welcome man's pent-up rage and hatred against the cruelty of his destiny. He accepts men even in all their unacceptability and unacceptingness. By so doing (or rather, by man's realisation of what God has

[3] N. W. Clerk, *A Grief Observed* (1961); p. 25.

done) he draws the sting of their hate. Man's unconscious grudge against life, against himself, and against God exhausts itself on the cruciform figure of the tortured and dying Christ. Here hatred runs out into the sand. As Jesus' death was the gateway to renewal of life through what we call the Resurrection, so also troubled men who pour out their hidden jealousy and spite and rage against God at the foot of the Cross find that at this very point they are standing on the threshold of that new life in Christ of which the New Testament so often and so eloquently speaks. Man can again begin to love, once he is assured, in the depths of his being, that the Being who created and sustains him really does love him with an everlasting love. Acknowledgement of the divine love becomes no longer an ecclesiastical formula, or a conscious avowal from which a man's unconscious self revolts: it is rather the expression of experienced reality. And it is only when a man experiences such love that he is free to respond with his own love. The psychic structure of our personalities is such that only by responding to love do we have the necessary feeling of security to be our natural selves without internal disharmony and tension. Since internal disharmony results in man's involvement in the " deadly sins ", it follows that the way of release from these sins is through the conscious and unconscious security which assurance of God's love alone can give.

I have tried, in these last few minutes, to give an interpretation of the Atonement which has meaning and power for to-day.[4] I cannot say much more than that this has meaning and power for me. I am sure that it does not meet the needs of everyone. I am equally sure that it does not fully meet the needs of anyone; for we are all of us much more complex individuals than my analysis would imply. The question, however, that I want to ask is this: is it a valid translation of the total biblical picture of redemption?

At first sight the answer would seem to be completely negative. For the presupposition of biblical imagery is that man is responsible for his predicament, both by his own actual sins and by his involvement in the primal sin of Adam. The Atonement is presented as the interpretation of an act by which the Merciful Judge restores men to a relationship with himself which they have forfeited by their own fault. In the interpretation, however, which I have just sketched the Atonement is the answer not primarily to

[4] I am glad to pay tribute to Dr. Frank Lake for his help in my understanding of the meaning of Jesus' death.

God's accusation against men, but to the Great Accusation of men against God.

The difference of viewpoint stems primarily from a difference in the concept of sin. If sin is something for which man is wholly responsible, then the interpretation which I have suggested cannot possibly be right. But if it is true that man's sins stem from his basic insecurity, often derived from childhood states before he was a responsible human being; if it is true that man's basic fault is usually hidden from his eyes by unconscious motivation because he cannot bear to face his agonising situation; then man cannot wholly be blamed by God for his sins. Indeed man's attempts at self-justification, his retreat and withdrawal from personal relationships, and his futile attention-seeking behaviour are all semi-automatic responses to his predicament; and the resulting "sinful" attitudes almost inevitably follow. It is therefore "natural" that man should rage against his Creator, even if his rage becomes inverted into hardly recognisable substitutes. It is true that, after man has been brought to himself by the realisation that his Creator really loves and accepts him despite outward appearances, he will be "sorry" for his previous imbalance and the suffering that he has caused both himself and those with whom he had to do. But he will not continue to feel " guilty " because he will know that guilt-feelings are the result of inner disharmony rather than the divine summons to self-abasement and self-hatred. For him the path will not lead from sin through guilt to joy. On the contrary, the joy of release will come first, leading to regret and sorrow that earlier bondage caused his relationships with God, with men and with himself to be so negative and bad.

Once it be granted that there is a radical difference between the biblical view of sin and that which psychology makes tenable to-day, is it possible then to say that the interpretation of the Atonement which I have sketched above is a valid one? I cannot see why not. So far as I understand it, the essence of the total biblical picture is that God, through the event of Christ, came to the help of mankind. He did not merely manifest himself: his self-disclosure was a costly act which potentially gives life to all mankind. It was a humble, compassionate, loving act, a self-emptying whereby God not only assumed complete humanity, but also suffered the worst that men could do. "He became sin for us." "He became a curse for us." The writers of the New Testament would not have dared to accuse God of injustice and indifference to the human situation. "Who are you, O man, to answer back to God? Will what is moulded say to its

moulder, ' Why have you made me thus?' '' asks
Paul. But Paul's very horror of such blasphemy
suggests that unconsciously he was asking this
very question. The Atonement as the answer
to man's Great Accusation against God belongs to
the twentieth century; but this thought is not
so far removed as it might seem from the unconscious thoughts and fears of the first century.

I should not however wish to suggest that
the interpretation of the Atonement which I have
given is the only one valid for to-day. It has
been suggested earlier in this lecture that the
doctrine of each age is conditioned to a certain
extent by its ideology. But this is not the whole
of the story. A person's theology is conditioned
to a certain extent by his own temperament. Differences of doctrine are not only due to differences
of environment or of intellectual power. If that
were so, two theologians, working in the same
environment, and gifted with the same intellectual
talents, would arrive at the same doctrinal formulations. But they don't; and the reason
for this is at least in part their differing temperaments affecting their formulation of doctrine.

When a young man comes up to me and tries
to persuade me that, unless I accept the Atonement doctrine of substitutionary punishment, I
am not a Christian, I realise that he is unconsciously so insecure about his convictions that he

feels the need to impose them on someone older
than himself. But I must be careful not to do
likewise. I dare not say to him: " Unless you
hold the particular interpretation of the Atonement which I hold, you are not a Christian."
For he plainly is a Christian. He finds new life
through Christ, and he is caught up into the life
of the Christian Church as much as (if not more
than) myself. I do not doubt that he is a sick
man. He is obsessed by guilt; and the only way
that he can find release from his guilt-feelings
is by means of his doctrine of substitutionary
punishment; and deep down he has not really
found full release by this mode, or he would not
be seeking to impose his solution on me with
such vehemence. But then we are all, to a greater
or less extent, sick men. If it were not so, we
should all be in perfect relationship with God,
with our fellow-men, with ourselves. God does
not, as it were, refuse to deal with that young man
until he is psychologically healthy. He does not
insist on a cure in a psychiatric clinic before he
can help us by the Cross of Christ. This would
be a new form of gnosticism! So long as that
young man remains in his present psychological
state, the doctrine of substitutionary punishment
remains the right and valid interpretation of the
Atonement for him. It is no good trying to
persuade him that his doctrine is wrong: indeed,

to do this would be to destroy his Christian faith. It is right—for him. What needs changing is his psychological state; and often the grace of Christ provides the self-knowledge which acts as the necessary medicine. But not always. In bad cases psychiatric treatment of some sort may be necessary and the resulting way of self-knowledge is often more painful than the guilt-feeling which it seeks to cure.

I have taken as an example the doctrine of substitutionary punishment. It is the same with other interpretations. For some, the Atonement must be understood in terms of sacrifice; for them the imagery of sacrifice, with its ingredients of death and representation and symbolic action, suits the needs of their psychological temperament. For others, God's nature must be predominantly not love but justice; and so for them a juridical doctrine of the Atonement is a necessary way of understanding God's act in Christ. Their understanding of God as justice is due both to their inborn temperament and to the early experiences of their childhood rather than to a purely intellectual process of ratiocination. Again, the concept of satisfaction, so popular in the middle ages, suggests a neurotic preoccupation with anger and hatred and a desire to placate by giving satisfaction to the angry party. It implies the attribution to God of a psychological process of appeasement which those who hold such a theory have probably experienced in their own selves. For such disordered folk the "satisfaction" theory of the Atonement is a valid and necessary means of interpreting it: indeed, without it, they could not appropriate the benefits of Christ's passion. As a final example, the Moral Influence theory of the Atonement may be cited. This theory interprets the atoning work of Christ by the analogy of education. The spectacle of God's love incarnate on the Cross draws out the best in man, and educates him to realise his full nature. Man must needs imitate the best when he sees it, according to this interpretation. This is, in fact, not always the case. Man often does not imitate the best that he sees. Were this so, the world would not have witnessed the Bulgarian atrocities and the Nazi terrors and the Indian massacres. Nevertheless, those who hold the "moral influence theory" are usually people who cannot progress under compulsion. For them the vision of God's love manifested on the Cross is more ennobling than an interpretation which involves a sub-personal transaction.

The total idea of Atonement which I am here suggesting seems at first sight purely relativistic. It would seem that any interpretation of the Atonement will do that seems to suit a man's psychological outlook. In fact, I am not trying to put forward quite this. I suggest that God deals with people as they are, not as they should be. (After all a perfect human being would have no need of Atonement—Jesus did not.) We do not have to be psychiatrically cured before we can benefit by the Cross. The " facts " of Jesus' life and death and resurrection and the experience of the Spirit remain constant for faith. New life through the event of Jesus is a continuing experience for members of the Church. These are constants. The interpretation of these " facts " depends partly on the ideology of the Church at a given period, and partly on the psychological temperament of the believer. The total biblical picture gives the norm of interpretation from which each generation, and each individual, must make his own translation. The adequacy of the translation must be tested both by its faithfulness to the " facts " and by its relevance and meaningfulness to the believer and by its lack of contradiction with the biblical imagery.

This course of lectures is concerned with the love of God. I have tried to suggest an interpretation of the Atonement which interprets the event of Christ as the vindication of the love of God. But I have tried also to suggest that this interpretation by no means exhausts the reconciling love of God. He loves his people so much that he communicates to them his new life by the

means most suited to their ability to receive it.
I am reminded of a perceptive review by Dr.
R. S. Lee of Dr. Paul Tournier's latest book,
The Strong and the Weak.[5] Dr. Lee criticises the
famous psychiatrist's over-simplifications which
by-pass the complexity of man's personality.
"The healing process," he writes, "is not in
the message of God's grace: it lies in Dr. Tournier
himself." Human personality, indwelt by God,
is in itself creative of healing. *A fortiori* the words
of Dr. Lee apply to Jesus. The healing power
of Jesus does not lie in a particular interpretation of the Atonement. It lies in Jesus himself.

[5] *New Society* (No. 40) 4 July 1963, p. 28.

THE CHURCH—"IN-GROUP" OR "OUT-GROUP"?

Earlier lectures in this course have been concerned with the love of God. By contrast this concluding lecture will take as its subject the love of neighbour. The latter springs from the former; in the words of Scripture, "the second is like unto it, namely this" (Matt. 22.39). It is not difficult to see why the one follows from the other. Since man is made in the image of God, he is "worth loving"; that is to say, he bears the divine imprint on his personality, and so he is an object of worth for his own sake. My neighbour as much as myself is the man for whom Christ died. If I love God, it is because I have first received his love; and I cannot keep this to myself. If his love is outward-looking, mine must be too. I must not "hog" the divine love. If God's love is poured out on my undeserving self, I must in turn give my love to others. Divine generosity evokes human self-giving.

The command for neighbourly love comes originally from the Old Testament. It is a part of what my Authorised Version calls "a Repetition of Sundry Laws" in Leviticus 19. The passage runs as follows:

> Thou shalt not hate thine brother in thine heart: thou shalt in any wise rebuke thy neighbour, and not suffer sin upon him. Thou shalt not avenge nor bear grudge against the children of thy people, but thou shalt love thy neighbour as thyself: I am the Lord. (vv. 17, 18).

The context makes it plain that by neighbour is meant "the children of thy people", i.e. a fellow-Israelite. The Hebrew word *reah* confirms this meaning.

We must next ask ourselves how the Rabbis understood this word *reah*. Did they understand by it anyone who happens to be a neighbour, or did they take it in its strict biblical meaning? I think that my cousin, Dr. C. G. Montefiore, has carried out the most recent investigation into this matter, and I give you his conclusions. He wrote that scholars

> have, I think, shown that the Rabbis understood "Reah" in the Pentateuch to mean the Jew or Israelite only. The *Reah* excluded the non-Israelite. It has however to be borne in mind that the majority of texts cited by Strack Billerbeck and others are specifically legal. . . . The Rabbis were well aware that a given action which constituted, according

to the Pentateuchal Law, a tort or wrong
between Jew and Jew might and obviously
did constitute a moral wrong between the
Jew and the foreigner.[1]

Dr. Claude Montefiore's final conclusion is as
follows:

The truth is that the Rabbis are not entirely
of one mind on the matter of loving or hating
the non-Jew. It would be unjust to sum up
the matter by saying that the Rabbis generally taught that it is right or permissible to
hate the Gentile. On the other hand, it would
be hardly less unfair to say that the Rabbis
taught that the love which was to be shown
to the Jewish "neighbour" was to be extended equally to all men, whatever their
race or nationality or creed.

The Rabbis saw the great importance of the
command for neighbourly love in Leviticus, and
they generally understood it in the sense in which
it is intended in the Bible. Rabbi Akibah, for
instance, the great Jewish martyr of the Second
Revolt, said of "Thou shalt love thy neighbour
as thyself": "This is the greatest principle in
the Law" (Sifra 89b). Even in the time of Jesus,
a scribe is reported to have said: "To love
God with all the heart and with all the under-

[1] *Rabbinic Literature and Gospel Teaching* (1930),
pp. 60-104.

standing, and with all the strength, and to love
one's neighbour as oneself, is more than all
whole burnt offerings and sacrifices " (Mark
12.33). The combination of the two Great Commandments is not even original to Jesus. It is
first found in the Testaments of the Twelve Pat-
riarchs (Testament of Iss. 5.2; Testament of
Dan. 5.3).

There can be little doubt that the early Church
believed Jesus to have summarised the whole law
in these two Great Commandments. There are,
as we might expect, marked divergencies of detail
in the various synoptic accounts of the occasion
when Jesus gave his summary of the Law (Mark
12.28-34; Matt. 22.34-40; Luke 10.25-27). We
may note, too, that the command for neighbourly
love appears in Matthew's version of the incident
of the rich young ruler (Matt. 19.19) but not in
the other two versions (Mark 10.17-22; Luke
18.18-23). The early Church plainly believed
that Jesus made this twofold summary of the
Law. It is most probable that he did so, for
this summary fits in with Jesus' teaching as a
whole.

There is a vast difference between Jesus' teaching on neighbourly love and the Rabbis' interpretation of Lev. 19.18. " Jesus intends above
all to disengage the idea of ' neighbour ' from
every relation of ' proximity ', whether of

family, friendship, or nationality. If he uses the traditional term, it is because it lends itself perfectly to this extension. . . . The neighbour, in Christian language, is Man."[2]

For Jesus, to love your neighbour may mean to love your enemy. "You have learned that they were told, 'Love your neighbour, hate your enemy.' But I tell you this: Love your enemies and pray for your persecutors" (Matt. 5.43f.; Luke 6.27). For Jesus, too, to love your neighbour may mean to love the despised alien; for according to Luke, Jesus told the parable of the Good Samaritan in answer to the question " And who is my neighbour?". The parable does not, of course, directly answer this question, but it does give a concrete instance of neighbourly conduct.

Jesus gives a theological reason for the extension of the idea of neighbour to include all in need. If men are to be children of God, they must imitate God. "Only so can you be children of your heavenly Father, who makes his sun to rise on good and bad alike, and sends the rain on the honest and the dishonest" (Matt. 5.45). Indeed Jesus shows that it is normal to show natural affection, and that there is nothing remarkable about it.

[2] C. Spicq, *Agapé dans le Nouveau Testament* (1958) vol. i, p. 183.

If you love only those who love you, what credit is that to you? Even sinners do that much. Again, if you do good only to those who do good to you, what credit is that to you? Even sinners do as much. And if you lend only where you expect to be repaid, what credit is that to you? Even sinners lend to each other, if they are to be repaid in full. But you must love your enemies and do good; and lend without expecting any return; and you will have a rich reward: you will be sons of the Most High, because he himself is kind to the ungrateful and to the wicked. Be compassionate as your Father is compassionate. (Luke 6.32-36; cf. Matt. 5.43-48.)

The same point is made in the saying about the dinner party, when Jesus' host is exhorted to entertain those who have no means of repaying his hospitality (Luke 14.12-14). In the Parable of the Sheep and the Goats the point is taken further. According to this parable, the criterion at the Last Judgement will be whether a man has lived up to the commandment to love his neighbour as himself, and the neighbours there are the hungry, the thirsty, the strangers, the ill-clad and the prisoners (Matt. 25. 31-45).

Jesus' teaching about the primary importance of neighbourly love was continued in the Church,

notably by St. Paul. But already a subtle change
in the meaning of neighbour can be noted. For
Paul neighbour means primarily a fellow-member
of the Christian Church. Jesus' illustration of
neighbourliness was an outcast Samaritan; but
Paul's image of neighbourliness was a redeemed
Christian community. Thus Paul, like his Master,
said that all the commandments are summed up
in the one rule: "Love thy neighbour as thyself"; but he made it clear that neighbour here
means a church member: "Leave no claims
outstanding against you, except that of mutual
love" (Ro. 13.8f.). When Paul was writing to
the Galatians he gave the same teaching. "The
whole Law," he wrote "can be summed up in a
single commandment: Love your neighbour as
yourself" (Gal. 5.14). Yet here, as in the Epistle
to the Romans, he made it absolutely clear that
"my neighbour" is a fellow-Christian, for he
wrote in the same passage of the letter: "Be
servants to one another in love."

Jesus said that we must help our enemies in a
disinterested way; but Paul said that we should
do it from self-interest—for "by so doing you
will heap live coals on his head" (Ro. 12.20).
Not that a Christian should ever behave badly
to anyone. Far from it. "Never pay back evil
for evil" Paul wrote to the Romans (Ro. 12.17).
Christians should use good so as to defeat evil

(Ro. 12.21). Never must a Christian pay back wrong for wrong to anyone (1 Thess. 5.15). Indeed Paul could even write: " Let all you do be done in love " (1 Cor. 16.14). But there was a kind of double standard. A Christian must give first priority to his fellow-Christians: then, if there was as it were an overflow, let love be shown to others. There was a distinction made between love to fellow-Christians and love to other people. " May the Lord make your love mount and overflow towards one another and towards all ", Paul wrote to the Thessalonians (1 Thess. 3.12); and in the second letter he echoed the same thought: "Always aim at doing the best you can for each other and for all men " (2 Thess. 5.15). Even the great hymn on love in 1 Cor. 13 is concerned with fellow Christians. "Love is the best way of all "—within the Christian community (1 Cor. 12.31). Once again let me quote Spicq, who has made the most recent and comprehensive study of love in the New Testament. He writes: "Paul envisages this charity almost exclusively within Christian communities, and when he mentions enemies or those outside, it is by pure reference to the Sermon on the Mount."[3]

It might seem that I am trying to contrast Paul's Epistles with the Gospels, and indulge in

[3] *op. cit.*, vol. ii, p. 296.

the false alternative of "Jesus or Paul", so typical of liberal Protestant thinkers at the turn of the last century. In fact, so far as neighbourly love is concerned, Jesus' teaching is more nearly taken over by Paul than by any of the other writers of the New Testament.

I will illustrate this statement by reference to three non-Pauline Epistles, and by reference to St. John's Gospel. Take first the Epistle to the Hebrews. There neighbourly love is actually called *philadelphia*, love of the brethren (He. 13.1). When the author writes, "We ought to see how each of us may best arouse others to love and active goodness" (He. 10.24), he is again referring to love of the brethren, for he is writing about the effect of corporate worship on the Christian congregation.

The same identification of neighbour is made in the Epistle of St. James. The command for neighbourly love in Lev. 19.18 is quoted in this Epistle, and it is called "the sovereign law". It follows Jesus in teaching that this law applies to those who are in material need; but "the brother" or "the sister" in need are fellow-members of the Christian community (James 2.15f.).

In the First Epistle of St. Peter the distinction of attitude towards Christians and non-Christians is clearly made. The Christian must, of course, conduct himself properly with everyone. If Christians behaved well to a pagan, they would no longer be maligned, but they would be seen to live good lives; and so God would be glorified (1 Peter 2.12). The constituted authorities must be obeyed. The Christians' good behaviour should silence the ignorance and stupidity of pagans. But this behaviour expresses an attitude different from that active love which Christians should show towards each other. " Give due honour to everyone; love to the brotherhood, reverence to God, honour to the sovereign " (1 Peter 2.17).

It is in the Fourth Gospel that the distinction of attitude towards Christian and non-Christian is most clearly marked. Christians are there, of course, ordered to imitate their Master, but in the Fourth Gospel Christ does not pray for the world, only for his disciples and those who will believe through them. In the Fourth Gospel Christ does not die for the world. He lays down his life for his friends; and his friends are defined as those who do whatever Christ commands them (John 15.14.). Jesus " had always loved his own who were in the world, and now [at his passion] he was to show the full extent of his love " (John 13.1). This love of Jesus for his disciples must lead to reciprocal love among the disciples. "I give you a new commandment: Love one another. As I have loved you, so you are to love one another" (John 13.34). Indeed, in one of the Johannine Epistles, it is even said that a man cannot love God unless he loves his fellow-Christians (1 John 4.20), while anyone who loves the world is a stranger to God's love (1 John 2.15).

From the synoptic gospels to the Johannine literature we have moved from one extreme to the other. In the synoptic gospels reciprocal love is depreciated and contrasted with the love that gives to anyone in need without hope of reward. In the Johannine literature it is forbidden to love anyone outside the closed circle of the Christian community; the "new commandment" is for reciprocal love within the Christian fellowship.

So far I have only been concerned with expounding New Testament texts. Let us now turn to the reasons which caused this alteration in the meaning of the word neighbour in the command "Thou shalt love thy neighbour as thyself".

In the first place, the early Christians found that because they were so closely identified with Christ, they were bound closely to one another. They called this experience the fellowship (or more accurately, the sharing) of the Holy Spirit. They were united to one another because they were united to Christ. This joyous and intense experience of " togetherness " was a gift of God. It was part of the privilege of being a Christian. It was a real experience of Christian love. Since this gift of mutual love was God-given, it is understandable that neighbourly love became introverted within the Christian congregation.

In the second place, the early Christians believed that the world was evil. It would soon come to an end. It was already in process of passing away. Christians were already living in the new world-order, which was shortly to be universally established. The death and resurrection of Christ meant that the first stages of the new world order had already been accomplished. Through Christ men might be saved from the old world order and transferred into the new order which Christ has inaugurated. It seemed to follow therefore that the best way of showing neighbourly love to non-Christians would be to preach the gospel to them, so that they might escape coming destruction. Naturally one's behaviour towards them must always be correct, so that no offence be given and calumnies be stopped. Their greatest need was salvation. The day of reckoning was so near that this need must take priority over all their other needs.

Fellow-Christians must be loved; but non-Christians must be offered salvation.

A third factor facilitated the shift in the meaning of neighbourly love. The primitive Church used the Old Testament Scriptures in its search for self-understanding. St. Paul, for example, without any sense of innovation, speaks of the Christian Church as the seed of Abraham and the Israel of God; and the author of 1 Peter calls it the People of God. In the Old Testament, Jews were exhorted to love their fellow-Jews as themselves. What could be more natural than that Christians, under the new dispensation, should understand the command to mean that Christians should love their fellow-Christians? That which was restricted to a national group was now to be contained within a religious group.

A fourth factor must also be admitted. The primitive Church found itself in a situation very different from that in which Jesus carried out his public ministry. Jesus was teaching and preaching within the confines of the Jewish people. The Jews firmly believed in One God, and they were trying, perhaps harder than any nation has ever tried before or since, to live to the glory of God. But the primitive Church found itself often as a small group of believers, often living in the midst of hostile neighbours, often surrounded by polytheistic pagans or by Jews who thought that

Christians were blasphemers. Within this situation the primitive communities would have been lost unless they had built up their own loyalties and concentrated on the strengthening of the Christian group.[4]

The difference between the teaching of the synoptic gospels and the rest of the New Testament on the meaning of neighbour is deep and profound. First, there is a theological difference. Jesus taught that men must imitate their heavenly Father who gives gifts to men without respect of persons. The early Church believed itself to be united in Christ, and this unity was such that the believers were specially united to each other. As members of the household of God, they had mutual ties of affection. As members of the Body of Christ, they were mutually dependent. As part of the structure of which the building of God was comprised, they were mutually supporting. It remains to be seen whether the two different theologies of love can be harmonised into a single whole.

There is also a strategic difference. The Church has often been compared to an army. An army has a function. Those who have served in the Forces may remember that an operation has an

[4] For a detailed examination of neighbourly love in the New Testament, see my article " Thou Shalt Love Thy Neighbour As Thyself ", *Novum Testamentum* v (1962), 157-170.

aim, intention and method. The aim of the
Church militant is—what? To make ready the
coming of the Kingdom, that is, the open acknowledgement of God as King? And if this is its
aim, what is the particular intention? Here
opinion divides. Some will say that the Church's
intention should be to draw men and women into
its ranks by preaching the good news of Christ,
until the Church becomes so large that it is co-
extensive with the world. In this case, the mis-
sionary work of the Church should be concentrated on the preaching of the Christian Gospel
to non-Christians. I use the word " concentrate "
advisedly: it is a military metaphor. If the
Church is to preach effectively, it must concentrate its forces into a compact, well-knit body.
Others, on the other hand, will say that as a
matter of strategy, practical love must precede
preaching, if the latter is to be effective. Others
will deny the use of strategy at all. It depends,
they say, on God's good pleasure whether or
not he uses the present members of his Church
to complete his kingdom. The task of the churchman, on this view, is to love his neighbours as
himself without calculating what the effect on
them will be. As he has freely received from
God, so he must freely give to others without
respect of persons.

Thirdly, there is a great pastoral difference of

approach involved in the two different meanings
given to "neighbour" in the command for neighbourly love. Should a Vicar visit "the faithful"
or the unchurched or both? Should a member of
the congregation join in as many as he can of
the multitude of parish activities with which he
is so often confronted? Is he called to love his
fellow-churchmen by helping them and sharing
with them, or is his first task to help *anyone* in
need, be he churched or unchurched? Should
a Church exercise responsibility for national welfare in a post-Christian society, or should it concern itself only with its own members? These
are very practical questions, bearing on ordinary
parish life. The difference in the meaning of
"neighbour" between the synoptic gospels and
the rest of the New Testament has implications
at the level of theology, church strategy and every-
day life.

Four factors were suggested for the shift of meaning between the synoptic gospels and the rest of
the New Testament of neighbourly love. These
factors seem less compelling in the twentieth
century than in the first century A.D. This is due
to our changed situation, our modified convictions
and our additional knowledge.

It is now generally realised that the intense
feeling of "togetherness", which the primitive

Church enjoyed, is not unique to Christianity. It is experienced by members of other religious groups who share a common purpose and a common life. In the New Testament the Holy Spirit is mentioned only as operative within the Church. But it cannot be maintained to-day that " the fellowship of the Holy Spirit ", in the sense in which the Church has understood the phrase, is found only within and among its members. Nor is this intense feeling of " togetherness " confined solely to religious groups. It is, for example, found among members of a Rowing Eight; and it was experienced by many during the last war in the fellowship of their service unit. In any case, the intense and joyous feeling of being united in and with Christ is not so marked in Christian communities to-day (apart from revivalist sects) as it was in the earliest congregations of the New Testament period. This is not necessarily because the earliest Christians were keener or better than contemporary Christians. A man's commitment and convictions cannot be gauged by the strength of the emotions which accompany them.

Just as the mode by which the Holy Spirit is normally experienced might seem to have changed, so also some convictions have altered. Few Christians now believe that the Second Advent of Christ is imminent; nor, on the whole, are they convinced that if non-Christians are not converted to Christianity in this life, they have forfeited their chance of eternal salvation. One of the results of these altered beliefs has been that Christians have no longer felt that they are required, by the urgency of the times, to concentrate on preaching the Gospel to non-Christians. They have felt able to have other kinds of relationships with them. Moreover it is no longer easy for a Christian to live apart from non-Christians. In our progressively more technological society, we are all becoming more dependent on each other. This affords more opportunities to the Christian to carry out works of love on behalf of the non-Christian as well as the Christian. This situation in turn has led many Christians to feel that non-Christians are more likely to listen without prejudice to the Gospel if Christians demonstrate to them by their acts of kindness the nature of Christian love. After all, members of a club may be expected to indulge in self-help and mutual support. Secular society provides many instances of this. But Christians, if they show love to non-Christians, can help to demonstrate that the Church is more than a club. The closer relationship between the Church and the world, rendered inevitable by the complexity and interdependence of modern society, has also led some Christians to learn from the world. They have discovered that, at any rate in a post-Christian society, Christian charity is not confined within the Christian Church.

Our church situation to-day is very different from that of Jesus or of the early Christians. Indeed, it is not uniform. It is different in Africa and Asia from what it is in Europe and America. It differs from town to country, and between city and city, nation and nation. It is unlikely, however, that a consideration of these differences will lead to a resolution of our problem. The meaning of neighbourly love is affected but not determined by the situation in which the Church finds itself. We must return to first principles.

God gives good gifts to all his creatures without respect of persons. In particular he bestows his wealth on human beings without reference to their individual worth. " He makes his sun to rise on the good and bad alike, and sends the rain on the honest and dishonest." Yet, despite universal benevolence God chose a particular people. The Jews were " the people he hath chosen for his inheritance ". This choice was not an election to privilege, but to service and (as their history shows) to suffering. The choice of the Jews did not diminish God's providential care for all. " The open consecration of a part marks the destiny of the whole " (Westcott).

As God dealt with the Jews, so Jesus with

his friends. For Jesus did have special friends.
He wept at Lazarus' death (John 11.35).
He called the Twelve primarily so that they
should be with him (Mark 3.14). For all
his teaching and preaching to the multitudes, for
all his healing work for individuals in need,
he lived in the common life of what has been
called "the first theological college of all".
They lived from a common purse (John 12.6)
and they shared a common table (Mark 14.14).
Jesus may have cut himself off from his own
family group, but he substituted for it another
group of those who, like him, gave up their lives
to the doing of God's will (Mark 3.32ff.). It
was on the basis of the intensive life of this "in-
group", that he was able to give himself exten-
sively to all who came to him in need. Jesus does
not seem to have tried to expand this inner
group " that he was able to give himself exten-
however, a rigidly defined and tightly closed
enclave. The confusion in the Gospels over the
names of the Twelve shows this. Moreover there
were other groups, almost shading into each
other; the "women who ministered to him of
their substance" (Luke 8.3), "those who were
round about him with the Twelve" (Mark 4.10),
the Seventy (Luke 10.1), the disciples and, on
the periphery, the multitudes.

The strength of family life shows the natural

need to belong to a group. Within the security
of the family group a child learns to accept and to
respond to love; and because of this early security, the child, when adult, can give love to
others. I might say that one must learn love
before one can give it to others; but this could
be misleading. For love is learnt not intel-
lectually but experientially. And a small group
is needed for this. Human beings are so constituted that they approach the universal through
the particular.

In Western society man naturally finds himself
in different groups. He belongs to a family, often
a small family unit consisting of husband and
wife and two or three children. He belongs too
to an extended family of relations, the ties of
which may be quite loose. There are the natural
associations of fellow-workers. There are clubs
or societies of like-minded members. There are
national groupings of country and international
groupings of a brotherhood of nations, such as
the British Commonwealth. The Church differs
from all these. It is a coming together of all
sorts and conditions of people because they believe
themselves to be called of God. The Church
is a voluntary association of different-minded individuals. Its members do not associate—or should
not—because of mutual self-interest, but to give
themselves to God. They do not join the Church

because this seems a better kind of club than others, but because they know that they are called to live to the glory of God by following in the steps of Christ. Within the Church they learn the love of God.

It is true that the love of God is mediated through the human love of a family. Yet Jesus' own relations with his family during his ministry suggest that family affection can be a bad guide to the Love of God. It may have to be foresworn. It can be easily introverted. Possessiveness can so easily masquerade under the guide of unselfish love. The Church is not itself free of such dangers; but in principle it should provide a group much more heterogeneous and of much greater variety than the natural unit of the family. Unlike the family, it owes its very existence to the desire of its members to respond to God's love.

You cannot learn love in large groups. But the world-wide Church consists of local congregations, and within these local communities there are often and there should always be smaller groups or cells. This is where the Love of God can be learnt. This is where the true meaning of the Two Great Commandments can be experienced. The Church is necessary if men and women are to learn and to live out lives of divine charity. The point may be put in many ways. Theologically, we must receive Christ from our fellow-Christians before we can show him to others. Sociologically, every out-group must first be an in-group. Psychologically, group therapy is the means of greater personal self-integration.

Unfortunately church groups have so often themselves been introverted. Reasons why this happened in the early Church have already been suggested; and although many of these reasons have lost their force to-day, others have taken their place. Shrinking congregations have made church groups withdraw into themselves. The advance of secular knowledge and the swift evolution of a technological culture have made church people fear that their Christian beliefs are no longer considered relevant to life; and fear has meant withdrawal. The theologians have speeded the process; for their exaltation of the doctrine of the Church, the product of the new "biblical theology", has seemed to give theological justification to a withdrawal which in fact has been largely motivated by suppressed fear.

In fact such a withdrawal is theologically incorrect. For it means that the Church is an end in itself, whereas in the New Testament it is not the Church but the Kingdom of God which is the regulative category of thought. The Church is here to minister to the Kingdom, as an anticipation of what the Kingdom will be like. To claim more for the Church is to twist biblical perspectives.

On the psychological level, this withdrawal can be seen to be due to fear. Perfect love casts out fear; but all too often men and women who have joined the Church have only paid lip service to God's love. Because they have failed to expose themselves to the love of God in the Cross of Christ, they are still sick in spirit. Genuine acceptance of the love of God leads to greater self-integration. There are still temptations to be faced and struggles to be won; but these are internal battles. It is no longer necessary to externalise that against which the struggle is being waged. It is no longer necessary to hate the enemy in order to be able to love " the in-group". It is no longer necessary for love to be exclusive. The Christian who has been enabled by the Love of God to reach a fair degree of self-integration will acknowledge that within the Church he has found the Love of God, and he will also feel forced to give expression to that love outside the Church. Freely he has received: freely he must give.

Many of the recent activities of the organised Church have given the impression that its members are preoccupied with themselves. No doubt canon law urgently needs revision. No doubt central and parochial finances need to be put on a proper businesslike basis. No doubt it is necessary to point out that the standards of the Church are very different from the standards of the world. No doubt the Mothers' Union, as an organisation of like-minded church women, has a perfect right to exclude from its membership whomsoever it wishes. No doubt it is perfectly proper to withdraw in order to advance. *Reculer pour mieux sauter* is an adage which has proved its worth in private as well as in corporate life.

Yet the impression given by many church activities is that the Church is an end in itself. It is becoming organisation-minded. A churchman joining a Christian congregation finds himself subjected to pressure to join one of its organisations. But the Church is not a mutual-help society with activities suited to different ages and groups, as " expressions of its common life ". As I have written elsewhere:

It is not here to run a parish welfare organisation, with masses of different outlets for people to ride their own hobby-horses of sanctuary creeping or running bazaars or ringing interminable and intolerable bells. I think that most church organisations obscure the meaning and function of the Church. The Church is not here to provide people with a sense of their own importance by doing church jobs. It is not here to fill

tragically empty lives with a sense of purpose
by running the ecclesiastical machine. It is
not here to allow people to indulge their
compulsive ritualisms or to find protection
from the blasts of the outside world. It is
neither a refuge nor a ritual nor a club nor a
coterie.[5]

No doubt men and women do need to belong
to societies of like-minded people who can cope
with their needs; and where the secular world
does not provide these, it is good that the Church
can offer them—so long as these do not inter-
fere with the Church's primary function, or with
the most important duties of its members. If lay
people have time over to organise themselves
into such groups, and if the local secular society
does not provide for their needs in this way, then
it would be foolish to bring such organisations to
an end. But it cannot be too strongly emphasised
that these organisations are not the main aim of
the Church, nor of the members who comprise it.
The Church is an anticipation of the Kingdom
and its mission is to prepare for its coming.
The Church is here to worship God. Its first
charge is obey the first Great Commandment. Because love can only be learnt in community,
it must fashion for itself a community (unless
one exists already) where love can be learnt.

[5] *Beyond Reasonable Doubt*, p. 35.

Then its members must go out into the world to show to others what they have so unworthily received. In home, office, factory, local government, club, association, school, and in every other aspect of life, it is the task of the Christian to glorify God by loving his neighbour. And his neighbour is not primarily his fellow Church member, but anyone in need whom he can help.

This will mean that the Christian must concern himself with justice as much as with charity; for there are many spheres of life where men can best love their neighbour by ensuring that justice is done to him, or where charity expresses itself in justice. It will mean that the Churchman goes out into the world to love people who often cannot return his love. It will mean breaking down barriers of mistrust and questioning the current standards of society. If the Christian goes out into the world he must not mind dirtying his hands, and he must not mind if he finds himself keeping company with people very different from himself. This is all part of what it means for a Christian to love his neighbour as himself. Of course a Christian will want to tell his neighbour the source of his love. He will tell him about the Good News of Christ. But there is no point in explaining the source of his love unless his neighbour can see it in action.

And what the individual does the Church as

a whole must do too. The Church must not only concern itself with its own canon law, but with the legislation of the whole country. It must ask fundamental questions about the aim, intention and practicability of measures before the legislative assembly of the country. It must be concerned with the conditions of society: it must look critically and sympathetically at the working of the Welfare State. It must take steps to bring to public notice classes of people who need help, and conditions of life which could be altered for the better. Not only individual churchmen but the Church as a whole should be outward looking as it strives to obey the divine command " Thou shalt love thy neighbour as thyself ". The Church must proclaim the Gospel of Christ over every department of the nation's life. But this proclamation will be hollow unless the Church humbles itself to be of service to the nation, and beyond national frontiers, to the world.

BIBLIOGRAPHY

The following books are suggested for further reading :

Chapter 1: The Great Accusation

F. R. Tennant, *The Origin and Propagation of Sin*, C.U.P. (1920)

J. S. Whale, *The Christian Answer to the Problem of Evil*, S.C.M. Press (1936)

C. S. Lewis, *The Problem of Pain*, Geoffrey Bles (1940), Fontana Books (1957)

N. W. Clerk, *A Grief Observed*, Faber and Faber (1961)

Chapter 2: The Sinlessness of Jesus

H. Rashdall, *Christ and Conscience*, Duckworth (1916) especially pp. 164-94.

L. W. Grensted, *The Person of Christ*, Nisbet (1933) especially pp. 271-86.

W. Temple, *Nature, Man and God*, Macmillan (1934)

Chapter 3: Atonement and Personality

J. K. Mozley, *Doctrine of the Atonement,*
Duckworth (1915)

V. Taylor, *The Atonement in New Testament
Teaching,* Epworth Press (1940)

P. Tillich, *The Courage To Be,* Nisbet (1952),
Fontana Library (1962)

H. A. Hodges, *The Pattern of Atonement,* S.C.M.
Press (1955)

*Chapter 4: The Church—" In-Group " or " Out-
Group "?*

E. F. Scott, *The Ethical Teaching of Jesus,*
Macmillan (1924)

J. Moffatt, *Love in the New Testament,* Hodder
& Stoughton (1929)

C. G. Montefiore, *Rabbinic Literature and Gospel
Teaching,* Macmillan (1930) especially pp.
60-104.

E. Brunner, *The Misunderstanding of the Church,*
Lutterworth (1952)

H. W. Montefiore, " Thou shalt love thy neighbour as thyself ", *Novum Testamentum* vol.
v (1962), pp. 157-70.

The ballad on page 14
is by Sydney Carter.